INSECTS

INSECTS

JOHN CLEGG

*Drawings by E. C. Mansell and
photographs by the author*

FREDERICK MULLER

First published in Great Britain 1957
by Frederick Muller Limited, 110 Fleet Street, London E.C.4

Reprinted 1962
New and revised edition 1969

S.B.N. 584-62021-7

Phototypeset by BAS Printers Limited, Wallop, Hampshire
Printed in Great Britain by Ebenezer Baylis and Son Limited
The Trinity Press, Worcester and London
Bound by Wm. Brendon & Son Ltd., Tiptree

Contents

Illustrations

1

What are insects?

However unobservant we are, we can hardly fail to notice insects. They force their presence on us everywhere we go. They bite us, they sting us, they get in our eyes or our jam, they eat our plants in the garden or our farm crops; they can give us, or our animals, dreadful diseases. On the other hand, some help to feed us, to clothe us (or at least our sisters), to pollinate our crops and, perhaps most important of all, help to keep down the numbers of their own kind. They exist in such abundance that they far outnumber all other groups of animals. Something like three-quarters of a million different kinds of insects have already been described and given names, and every year the museums of the world are adding hundreds to the list. In this country alone about 20,000 kinds are known already.

But, before we go any further, it will be as well to be quite clear that we know exactly what we mean by insects. Most people feel that they know an insect when they see one, but quite often they are wrong! A spider, for instance, is not an insect although it is often called one. Neither is a centipede or a millipede or a water-flea, although these creatures too are frequently mistaken for insects. How then can we distinguish an insect?

The name "insect" gives us a clue for it comes from the Latin word *insectum* which means "cut into" and refers to the way in which an insect's body is cut into or divided into sections, or segments as they are called. Then the body is separated into three distinct parts: the head, the thorax or chest and the abdomen (see diagram opposite). Attached to the thorax are (except in a very few insects) *three* pairs of legs and also, usually, wings. On the head are a pair of feelers or antennae. Now you will see why some of the other creatures mentioned above are not insects. Spiders, for instance, have *four* pairs of legs, their head and thorax are merged into one and they have no antennae. Millipedes and centipedes (myriapods) have many pairs of legs and show no separation between their thorax and abdomen. Water-fleas also have many pairs of legs, no separation between the head and thorax and two pairs of antennae.

These other creatures are *related* to insects because they share with them the possession of an outside skeleton or "shell" and jointed limbs. Because of this latter characteristic the whole group is given the name of Arthropoda (Greek *arthron*, a joint; *podos,* of a foot). The following summary will perhaps be useful to refer to:

Arthropoda.—Animals with a body divided into segments, jointed limbs and external skeleton.

Division 1.	Crustacea:	Two pairs of antennae. Water-fleas, barnacles, woodlice, shrimps, lobsters and crabs.
Division 2.	Myriapoda:	Single pair of antennae; numerous pairs of similar legs. Millipedes and centipedes.

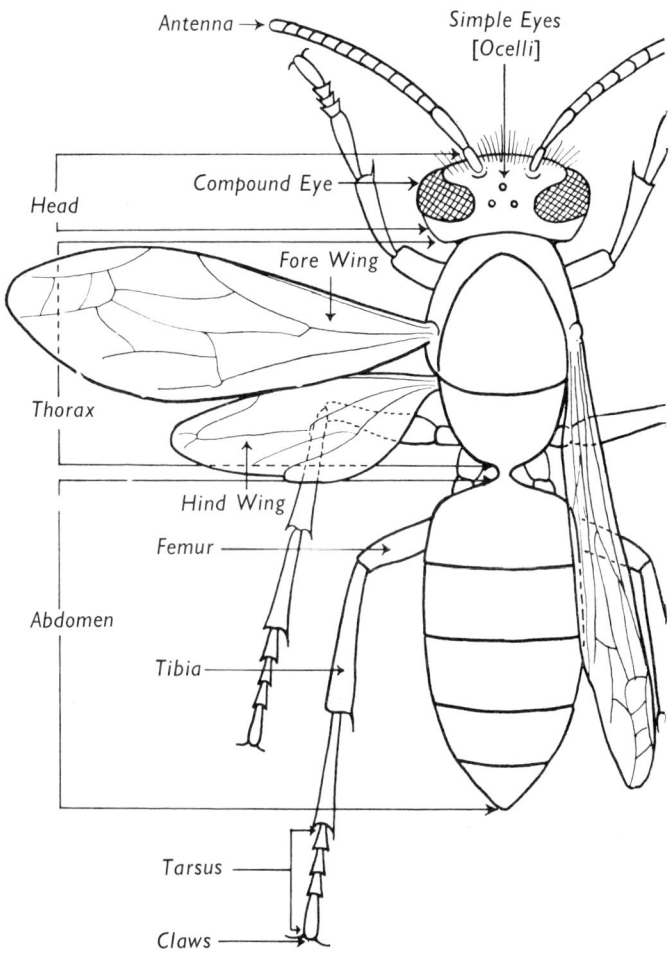

The parts of a typical insect

Division 3. INSECTA: SINGLE PAIR OF ANTENNAE; THREE PAIRS OF LEGS; USUALLY TWO PAIRS OF WINGS.

Division 4. Arachnida: No antennae; four pairs of walking legs.
Spiders, harvesters and mites.

You should note that the peculiar features of insects I have mentioned apply only to *full grown* or adult insects. One has only to think about a caterpillar to remember that the early stages of insects are usually quite unlike their parents and I am afraid there is no easy description that can be given of all the variations they show. We shall have to wait until we are dealing with particular insects before it will be possible to describe some of these immature stages.

Perhaps a few words ought to be said here about the skin or "shell" of insects, which as we have seen acts as an outside skeleton. It consists of three main layers, the inner two being flexible and elastic while the outer layer becomes extremely tough and hard after exposure to the air and will not stretch. This shell, which covers every part of the body, including the eyes and antennae, takes the place of the internal skeleton of bones which we have in common with all other backboned animals—fish, amphibians, reptiles, birds and mammals—and an insect's muscles are attached to this outside skeleton as ours are to our bones. In some ways this form of outside skeleton has advantages, but it has this great disadvantage: that when an insect is growing, its skeleton, or at least the outside layer of it, cannot grow with it, any more than your suit of clothes, when you grow too big for it, can get bigger. Like you, the insect when it grows has to get a new suit. Thus, during periods of growth, an insect must, at intervals, get out of its shell and make a new one. This is done by growing a thin, flexible skin inside the old one. In due course the old shell splits and the insect draws itself out in its new skin, still moist and flexible. The skin stretches and after a short exposure to the air becomes hard. This operation is called moulting and during the growth of a caterpillar may take place about nine times. Grasshoppers, however, moult only five times before they reach the winged stage and some insects that spend their early stages in water, such as mayflies and stoneflies, may moult as many as forty times. In some cases a moult may result merely in a larger version of the same creature as in the several moults of a caterpillar. On the other hand a stage totally unlike the last one may emerge as when a caterpillar changes into a chrysalis or a chrysalis into a butterfly.

Once an insect has become adult it does not grow, or moult, any more. Little flies do not grow into big flies; if we see little flies we can be sure they are different kinds or species.

2

The kinds of insects
and how they are classified

Scientists have divided the whole of the animals and plants in the world into groups, choosing features in each animal or plant which clearly relate it to other members of the same group. Thus we have already seen that water-fleas, woodlice, crabs, millipedes, spiders and insects are included in a group called the Arthropoda or "jointed-limbed animals" because they all have certain features in common. Such a large group is called a PHYLUM (plural phyla) and a phylum is further subdivided into various CLASSES of which *Insecta*, the insects, is one. Classes are composed of ORDERS, and it is the various orders of insects that we must now consider. Originally these orders were based on differences in the wings of insects and the scientific names which have been given to the different orders of insects are based on wing features as we shall see.

There are, however, often insects which even in the adult stage never have wings. They are small and not very important insects such as the silverfish which is sometimes seen running about on the floor or shelves of kitchens and pantries, and having mentioned them we can now forget them!

The rest of the insects which have wings, except in certain individual cases, can be divided into two categories: those that pass through four stages in their metamorphosis or life-history (egg, larva, pupa and adult); and those that have only three stages, leaving out the pupa stage. A butterfly or a moth is a good example of the first category. From the egg hatches a larva (which we call a "caterpillar") whose sole function in life is to eat and grow. Eventually, when it has moulted several times, it changes into a pupa ("chrysalis") often making a shelter ("cocoon") in which to rest. For the pupal stage is a resting period to enable the insect to carry out those striking *internal* changes, including the development of wings, which result in the eventual emergence of the perfect winged butterfly or moth from the old pupal skin.

Such a series of changes is called a *complete metamorphosis*, but some orders of insects undergo an *incomplete metamorphosis* (see illustration below). From the egg emerges a kind of larva, usually called a "nymph", that does not differ very much in appearance (although it does, of course, in size) from its parents. It feeds, moults and grows but never undergoes a resting stage, and if examined closely the larva

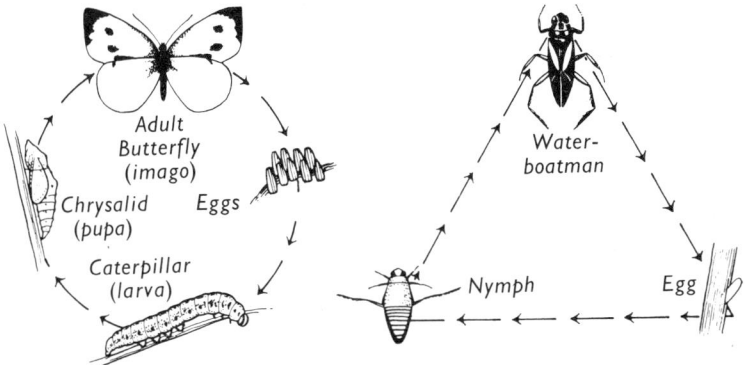

Metamorphoses of insects. The left diagram shows the four stages of a complete metamorphosis; the right one shows an incomplete metamorphosis where the pupal stage is omitted

will be seen to have buds of wings developing *outside* its body. In due course, and quite suddenly, the skin of the larva splits and the fully developed insect emerges.

These differences in metamorphosis give us a convenient feature of classification and, in a similar way, other characteristics—wings with scales, wings with hairs, wings changed into hard cases and so on— enable us to divide the great number of different kinds of insects into the following orders:

WINGED INSECTS, WITHOUT PUPAE, WINGS DEVELOPING OUTSIDE THE BODY

Cockroaches, grasshoppers, crickets. Order Orthoptera
    (*orthos,* straight; *pteron,* a wing)
The front pair of wings of these insects is leathery and serves as a cover for the hind pair which is transparent and usually folded neatly. To this order belong also the locusts, which are really large grasshoppers.

Stoneflies. Order Plecoptera (*plekein,* to fold)
These insects are found near streams and rivers in which their larval stages are passed. Both pairs of wings are transparent.

Earwigs. Order Dermaptera (*derma,* skin)
Although earwigs rarely fly they have large and beautiful wings folded under the skin-like fore wings.

Mayflies. Order Ephemeroptera (*ephemeros,* living for
    a day)
Like the stoneflies, these insects live mainly near running water. The adults live only sufficiently long to pair and lay eggs—in some kinds a few hours.

Dragonflies. Order Odonata (*odous*, a tooth)—*a reference to the sharply-toothed jaws of the adults*
There are two types of dragonflies: the large and powerful true dragonflies and the delicate damselflies. Both have nymphs which live in ponds and ditches.

Termites. Order Isoptera (*isos*, equal, similar)
Although popularly called "white ants", termites are unrelated to true ants and resemble them only in living in social communities. Termites are not found in Britain.

Book-lice. Order Psocoptera
Although some members of the order have wings, the best-known ones, which are nuisances in libraries, are wingless.

Lice. Order Anoplura (*anoplos*, unarmed; *oura*, a tail)
These somewhat revolting creatures are insects which are now wingless although it is believed their distant ancestors had wings which became useless when they adopted a parasitic life on other animals.

Thrips. Order Thysanoptera (*thusanos*, a fringe)
Thrips are very tiny insects which live in flowers. Their two pairs of wings bear lovely fringes of long hairs but, of course, they can only be seen under a microscope.

Bugs. Order Hemiptera (*hemi*, half)
Although most people use the word "bug" rather as a joke, it is the correct name for a large group of insects which include plant-bugs and water-bugs. They have beaks with which they suck the juices of their prey or plant food and the front pair of wings serves as a

15

leathery sheath for the hind pair. The name of the order is given because some kinds of bugs have *half* the front wings leathery and the tips transparent.

WINGED INSECTS, WITH PUPAE AND WITH WINGS DEVELOPING INSIDE THE BODY

Lacewings and *ant-lions*. *Order* Neuroptera (*neuron*, a nerve)
These insects are slenderly built but have long many-veined wings. Lacewings are common in gardens in summer. The larvae of ant-lions live in conical pits in sand into which their prey falls.

Alderflies and *snakeflies*. *Order* Megaloptera (*megas*, great, large)
Also with large, many-veined wings. Alderflies are found near still waters, their larvae being aquatic.

Scorpionflies. *Order* Mecoptera (*mekos*, length)
Like the previous orders, with which they were once classified, the scorpionflies have long, many-veined wings. The male holds the tail-end of its body over its back in a similar way to a scorpion.

Caddisflies. *Order* Trichoptera (*trichos*, of hair)
The larvae of these insects are caddis grubs which make protective cases of sticks, leaves, stones, etc., and are familiar to anyone who has hunted in ponds and streams. The adult insects resemble moths, but their wings are covered with minute hairs, not scales.

Butterflies and *Moths*. *Order* Lepidoptera (*lepis*, a scale)

16

The wings of butterflies and moths are covered with minute scales only visible, of course, under a microscope.

Beetles. Order Coleoptera (*coleon,* a sheath)
The front pair of wings (elytra) of beetles is hard and horny and acts as a sheath for the transparent hind wings which alone can be used for flying. Beetles form the largest group of insects and in fact outnumber in species every other similar group of animals.

Flies. Order Diptera (*di,* two)
Flies, such as the housefly, have only two pairs of wings, the hind pair having become so much reduced in size that they are now merely knobs and are used as "balancers". In addition to the familiar housefly, mosquitoes, midges and many other unpleasant insects belong to this order.

Ants, Bees and *Wasps. Order* Hymenoptera (*hymen,* a membrane)
Some insects in this order are wingless but when wings are present they are four in number, transparent and membranous and the front and back pairs can be hooked together. The feature that most of us remember about this order of insects is that many of them have stings!

3

The flight of insects

Although nearly all forms of movement—walking, hopping, crawling, burrowing, swimming and flying—can be undertaken by insects of some kind or other it is in flight that they excel. They are the most perfect flying machines on the earth and compared with them the bats, birds and, of course, man's aeroplanes put up a very poor performance. Sometimes they seem to defy all the laws of flight and during the 1939–45 war, with the object of stimulating workers in a well-known aircraft factory to work their hardest and overcome technical difficulties, a card was fastened on the wall which pointed out that by all the laws of aerodynamics (the science which treats of the principles of flight) a bumble-bee can't fly—but it does! And when the heavy, bulky body of a bumble-bee is considered in relation to its comparatively small wings, it does seem incredible that it can fly, and fly well.

Whereas the wings of birds and, among mammals, the bats started off by being structures for quite a different purpose than flight, insects' wings have been developed solely for that function and that perhaps explains why they are such efficient tools. We have to go a long way back in the history and development of animals to find out how their flying mechanisms developed but the story is quite clear if we examine fossil remains of, say, birds and insects. For some curious reason the fossil remains of bats are rare but, even so, one has only to look carefully at the wing of a present-day bat to see that it is really only a hand with skin joining the fingers; the skin also joins the fore-limb to the hind legs and the tail. It is not quite so easy to see that a present-day bird's wing is similarly formed from a kind of front claw, as some of the toes have now disappeared, but there is no doubt that it is so, as fossils show. With insects, however, the wings have always been wings and the earliest fossil insects known, which lived in the Carboniferous period of the earth's history—some 300 million years ago, at a time when all the coal we burn today was living plant life— have three pairs of wing-like structures. Although even at this early phase of their history at least two of the pairs of wings were well developed, it is believed that they had their origin much further back in time as perhaps simple flaps growing from the side of the body and probably only useful for gliding from place to place, much as the so-called flying squirrels do today.

Well, it's a far cry from those distant days and there is no denying that today the wings of insects are among the most beautifully-made structures in nature and, in conjunction with the muscles that control them, wonderfully efficient.

The wings of insects are extensions of the skin and when they are developing in, say, the chrysalis stage of a butterfly, they are like little bags or balloons, containing tubes or veins. When the butterfly emerges from the chrysalis skin it pumps liquid into the veins, thus stretching the bag to its utmost and the opposite sides come together to form a flat wing with a network of veins. After a short time the skin hardens and the butterfly can then fly away.

The next time you have the opportunity, examine carefully the wings of a dragonfly as it sits on some waterside plant on a summer's day. Notice the length of the wings, the marvellously thin membranes of which they are composed and the strong supporting network of veins, the patterning of which varies in each kind of dragonfly. Notice, too, that the veins across the wings are close together at the front or leading edge of the wing to give strength where the stresses are greatest in flying.

Dragonflies, and some other insects, move the front and back pairs of wings independently when flying and this was probably the way in which all the earliest insects flew. In the course of time, however, other groups of insects came to join the two wings of a side together and fly as if they had merely a single pair. The groups to which bees and wasps belong now have a series of small hooks on the front edge of each of the hind wings which can be fastened on to a fold on the rear edge of the front wing and, when setting off on a flight, the two pairs of wings are hooked together and used as one. Some moths have a simpler device on the hind wings which slips under a hook-like structure on the front wings.

Our common housefly and its relatives—the Diptera —have, as we stated on page 17, lost their hind wings altogether and they are represented only by knobbed "balancers". Nevertheless, these are of importance in flight and flies which have been deprived of them cannot keep their balance when in the air and tumble about like an aeroplane out of control.

As we noted in Chapter 2 there are other insects, including beetles and bugs, that use only one pair of wings, but in their case it is the hind wings that are of use in flight, the front· pair now being merely

Hawker Dragonfly resting after emerging from its nymphal skin.
(*Magnified*)

sheaths for the hind ones.

Incidentally it should be remembered that in insects the wings not only propel them through the air but steer them too, for they have no tail to act as a rudder or a brake as have birds and bats.

It is not an easy task to measure the wing beats of an insect, but it has been done by ingenious scientists using such methods as making an insect's wings rub against a rapidly revolving drum on which there is paper covered with soot. As the wings vibrate they rub off some of the soot and each beat leaves a mark or a curve. From such experiments some interesting results have been obtained. It is found, for instance, that a housefly makes nearly 200 wing beats *per second* and a bee as many as 250. At the other end of the scale, some butterflies only flap their wings about a dozen times per second and dragonflies from twenty to fifty times.

The speeds of flight of insects, as distinct from the number of wing beats, do not seem very striking if we measure them in miles per hour, as we are so accustomed to our jet aeroplanes doing several hundred miles an hour. But perhaps it is unfair to judge the speeds of such tiny flying machines as insects in our giant measurement of miles per hour. Expressed in feet per second and remembering that the length of most insects is merely an inch or so, their performance seems adequate: a dragonfly achieves about twenty feet per second, a housefly six feet and a bee nine feet.

To conclude this account of wings and flight, it may be mentioned that the females of some insects have lost the power of flight and even in some cases their wings altogether, although the males are quite normal. The beetle called the Glow-worm is one example and among British moths so are the Pale Brindled Beauty and the Vapourer. We do not know why these females have lost the power of flight, but it is interesting to find that they have all perfected some means whereby the males can search them out!

4

Breathing, smell, sight and hearing

I expect you know that in the higher animals, including ourselves, the air which is breathed in passes first into the blood which then carries it round the body to every part needing it. In insects this is not so. The air is taken in at air-holes, or *spiracles*, spaced at intervals along both sides of the body, and passes from them by means of much-branched air tubes, called *tracheae*, direct to every part of the body.

If you look carefully at a caterpillar you will see the little air-holes at intervals all along both sides of the body.

Up to a point this is a very satisfactory method of breathing but since it depends on the rate at which the air can pass along the breathing tubes, and this is rather a slow process, it is only satisfactory when the air has short distances to go. For this reason insects have always remained small creatures, or at least thin creatures. There were, in the Carboniferous period of the earth's history, giant dragonflies with a wing-spread of about two feet and there are today in the tropics giant stick insects about one foot in length. But both these groups of insects are thin-bodied so that the air taken in at the spiracles all along the body hasn't really very far to go. It is probably a good thing insects had this method of breathing. Had they

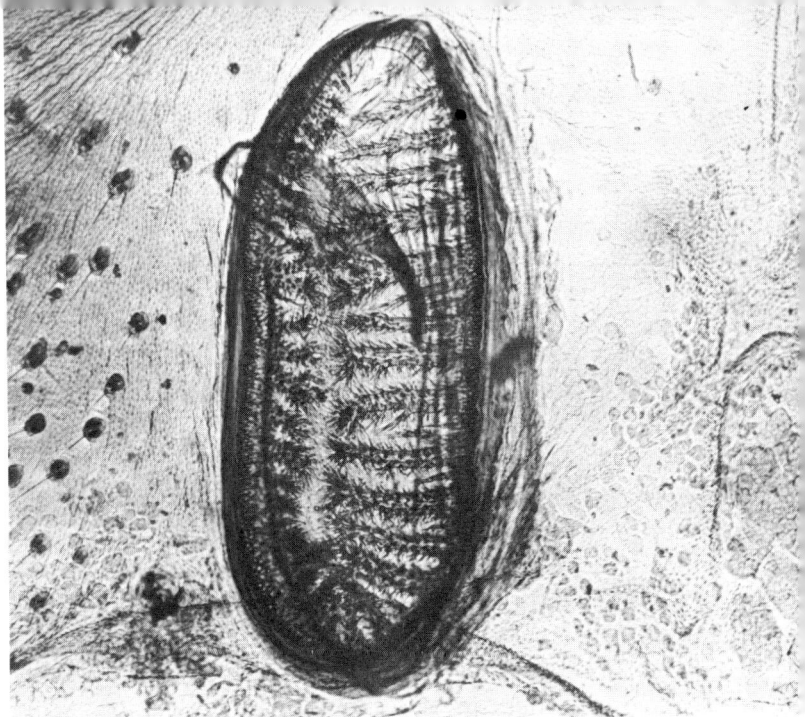

Spiracle of a beetle (*highly magnified*). The hairs around the opening keep out the dust in a similar way to the hairs in our own noses

Main trachea of a beetle (*highly magnified*). The rings of supporting material (chitin) are clearly shown

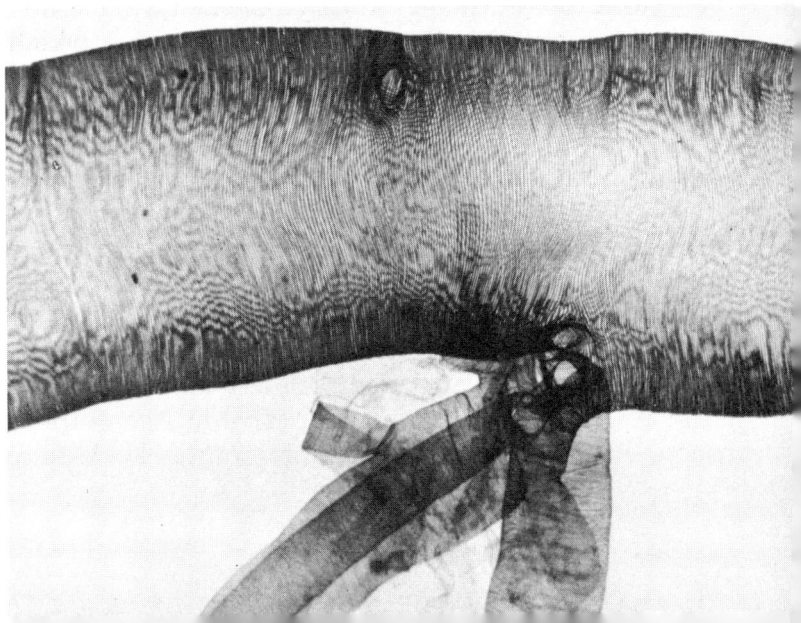

developed an efficient system such as we have with air contained in blood pumped round the body, there might have been no limit to the size they reached and beetles the size of elephants would soon have made short work of man and most of the other animals too!

SMELL

You are probably wondering how, if insects have no noses for breathing, they manage to find their mates or their food by smell. It is believed that the sense of smell is located in the "feelers" or antennae, and also in sensitive hairs or pores on other parts of the body. Under a microscope the feelers of a bluebottle fly for instance are seen to be covered with very tiny pits or pores and to the base of each of these a nerve passes. If the feelers are covered with grease or wax to seal these pores a bluebottle cannot find the decomposing meat on which it needs to lay its eggs, and it seems clear that they enable the insect to smell out the right conditions for its offspring to develop. The male Cockchafer, or May-bug, has very lovely antennae, the leaves of which can be opened out like a fan. Here again each section of the fan has an immense number of minute pits.

We know that some insects, at least, have an extremely sensitive sense of smell. In certain moths, as, for example, the Oak Eggar and the Vapourer Moth, the females have scent glands and the males locate their mates from a long way away purely by smelling them. Moth collectors imprison females of these species in little cages with muslin or gauze sides and place them by an open window. If conditions are right, there are soon clusters of males round the cage. By experiment it has been shown that the males of some species can pick up the scent at least as far away as a mile, and probably from greater distances.

The "feelers" do also act, as their name implies, as organs of touch and perhaps the two senses, touch and smell, are more closely allied in insects than they are in ourselves, particularly in ants and bees. When a worker from a colony of either of these groups of insects returns to the colony there is a great deal of stroking with the antennae, perhaps to make sure the new arrival is really a member of that colony, perhaps to find out the source of nectar or other food that the forager has located.

The antennae are often wonderful structures and a selection of different kinds is illustrated below.

SIGHT

Most adult insects have two kinds of eyes—simple eyes called ocelli, few in number and on the tops of their heads; and large compound eyes, sometimes occupying most of the two sides of the head, which are made

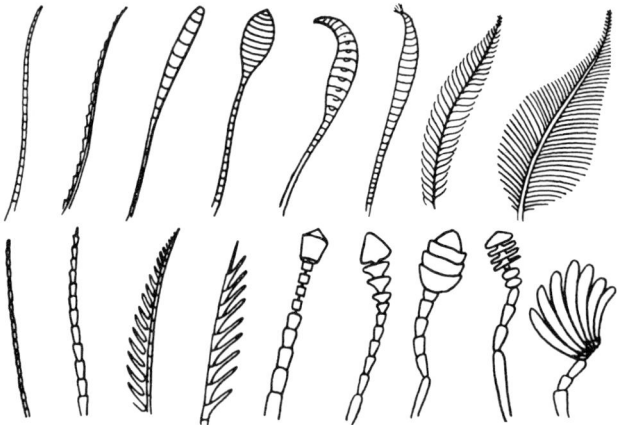

Types of antennae or feelers: *top* those of butterflies and moths, *below* those of beetles

up sometimes of many thousands of separate eyes. Some insects, however, have only one kind of eye and larvae may have none at all.

It is not quite clear what purpose the ocelli serve, but possibly they enable an insect to see close objects or to detect differences in the nature of the light during the day.

The compound eyes are some of the most wonderful structures in the animal kingdom. The separate lenses making up these compound eyes are arranged closely together just like the cells in a beehive and their number is sometimes enormous. A housefly has about 4,000 in *each* of its compound eyes and some dragonflies have 25,000 or more. Little wonder that insects are not easy to catch! The compound eyes, which are never more than two in number, are situated on either side of the head and often the whole head seems to be nothing but eyes! Whatever is seen with them, it is certainly not thousands of images of the same scene!

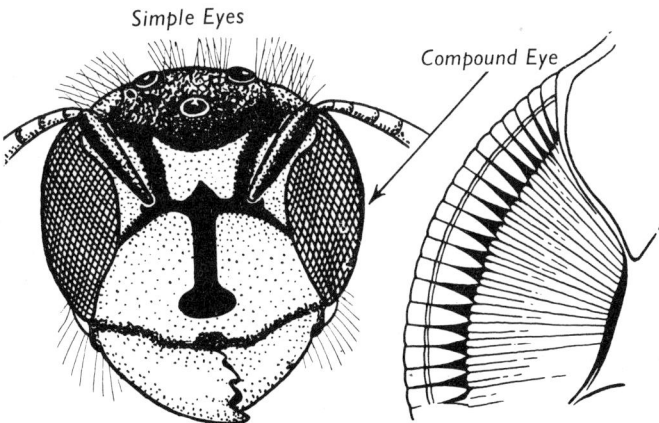

Simple Eyes

Compound Eye

The two kinds of insect eyes: on the left is the face of a wasp showing simple and compound eye, on the right is a section through a compound eye to reveal some of the tubular separate eyes of which it is composed

Some of the lenses in the compound eye of a beetle. (*Highly magnified*)

Each of the separate eyes making up the compound eye is a complete eye but is so constructed that it can see only what is *immediately* in front of it. It seems probable that the effect an insect gets is of a large number of tiny points of light and darkness depending on what was in front of each single eye. You have probably seen in a public building a floor, called a mosaic floor, in which a pattern or picture is made up of a great many pieces of differently coloured stone. The insect's surroundings must similarly be transmitted to its brain as a mosaic picture. Since its eyes cannot focus, the picture will probably be rather blurred and useful only in giving it a general view of its surroundings and—what is more important—giving warning of movements nearby, whether of enemies or prey.

SOUNDS AND HEARING

Can insects hear sounds? It seems certain that some, at least, can do so for they are provided with structures for *making* sounds and it would be strange if they were not able to hear them also.

Most insect noises are made by rubbing one part of their body against another, a method called *stridulation*. Everyone who has been in the country in summer must have heard the chirping of grasshoppers and crickets. This is a noise made mainly by the males and is obviously for the purpose of attracting the females. In species with long antennae—the crickets as they are called—the noise is produced by rubbing the leathery wing case of the right-hand side against that of the left. In short-horned grasshoppers, on the other hand, the legs are used for stridulation. On the part of the hind leg that corresponds to the thigh in higher animals there is a row of pegs and the insects draw these across the fore-wing.

Indoors, the chirruping of the house cricket is a familiar sound around the fireplaces of older houses or in other warm places.

It may seem a strange way to us to attract one's mate, but even human beings apparently find the chirping a pleasant sound. In parts of the world as far apart as Italy and Japan, grasshoppers, or their relatives the field-cricket, have been kept in little cages for their "songs", and the breeding and sale of the insects was at one time a thriving industry.

Each kind of grasshopper and cricket has a distinctive "song" and naturalists are usually able to identify the different British species by this feature alone. But the rate of chirping is more frequent in hot than in cooler weather and some people say they are able to tell the temperature by counting the number of chirps a cricket makes in a certain time. In their Penguin book, *The Weather*, the authors Raymond Bush and George Kimble give the following instructions: "Count the number of chirps (of a cricket) in fourteen seconds, add forty and you will have the temperature to within a couple of degrees, nine times out of ten."

Naturally, insects which produce sounds like this must have hearing organs to receive them. These

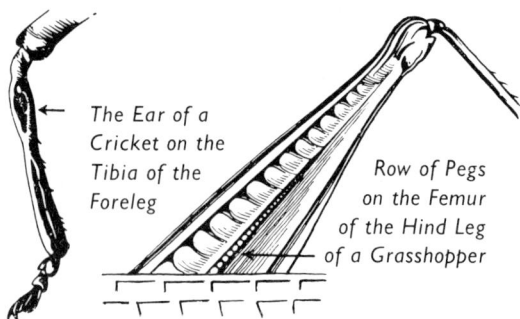

The Ear of a Cricket on the Tibia of the Foreleg

Row of Pegs on the Femur of the Hind Leg of a Grasshopper

The "ear" of a cricket and the sound-producing structures on the leg of a short-horned grasshopper

"ears" are often in strange places. In crickets they are placed on the shin (tibia) of the fore-legs (see above) but in grasshoppers they are on the body itself close to where the thorax and abdomen join. Both the males and females have "ears".

Other insects which make sounds are some beetles and bugs, including, rather strangely, some of the water-bugs, the lesser water-boatmen. They rub bristles on the inner surface of the femur of the front-legs against the edge of the head. No "ears" for receiving these sounds have so far been discovered, but they can probably be detected by members of the same species by other means as, for instance, by sensitive hairs which are known to be receptive to sounds and other vibrations in some insects.

Not all insect sounds are attractive or pleasant to us. Anyone who has been bitten by a vicious gnat or mosquito will have good cause to remember the high-pitched singing note which usually accompanies the attack. And the angry buzz of an attacking bee or wasp similarly will not bring back happy memories!

An insect sound which has long caused foreboding is the tapping of the Death-watch Beetle. The larvae of this insect often burrow in the structural timbers of old houses, churches and cathedrals. When the adult beetles emerge (usually about April) from the tunnels in which they lived as larvae, they tap repeatedly with their heads against the wood on which they are standing to attract their mates. In the stillness of an old house there is no doubt that this tap, tap, tap is a very eerie sound and it gave rise to an old superstition that the death of one of the occupants of the house was impending—hence the name given to the insect!

I dare say you are wondering if insects have brains. Well, they have a kind of brain which, like yours and mine, is situated in the head region. It is connected to a nerve cord which does not run down the back like ours but along the whole length of the body on the underside, or ventral region. Along its length there are swellings called "ganglia" (singular "ganglion") which control the parts of the body nearest them, so the brain does not have as much to do as ours and merely acts as a receiving centre for messages received from the sense organs—eyes, antennae, etc., and as co-ordinating centre directing the way the insect responds to the messages that have been received. Thus it is that an insect can carry on many of its activities even when its brain has been damaged or even lost altogether. If food is placed near the mouth the insect can eat it; if it is raised off the ground it can fly and so on. Lack of a brain merely prevents the insect from *starting* to do any of these things for itself.

5

Food and feeding

It will be as well, before going any further, to say a few words about the ways in which insects feed, for it is in their capacity as devouring demons that they are so important to us.

There are very few things indeed, plant or animal, that some insect or other has not tackled as food. Substances deadly to us such as strychnine are apparently relished by some insects. Others delight in the corks of entomologists' killing bottles! The dead bodies of birds and animals, photographic film, woollen clothing, old furniture, book bindings, whitewash and shoe-polish are only a few of the unpromising substances that are included in the diets of some insects.

The mouth-parts of insects are usually somewhat complicated structures and some of the forms they take are shown in the illustration opposite. Some insects have structures intended for biting and chewing solid food and then there are usually three kinds of jaws: the mandibles or principal jaws; the maxillae or accessory jaws and a third pair which are joined together to form a kind of lower lip, called the labium. Such mouth-parts are found in beetles, grasshoppers, earwigs and dragonflies.

Other insects take only liquid food and their mouth-

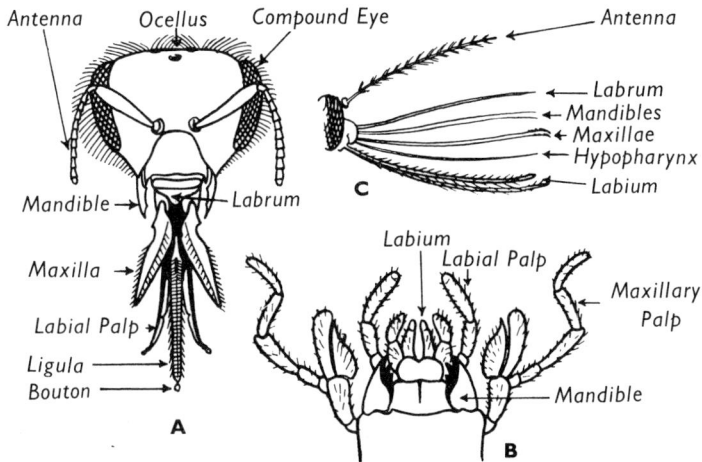

Mouth-parts of *A*, a bee, *B*, a cockroach and *C*, a gnat. The mouth-parts of the bee and the gnat are used for sucking up liquids, while those of the cockroach have biting jaws for chewing solid food

parts are changed so that they are suitable for sucking up plant juices, nectar or the blood of animals and if necessary for piercing their prey or host plant. Plant bugs, green-fly, butterflies and moths, houseflies and mosquitoes have such kinds of mouth-parts.

Some insects feed exclusively on animal food and are called *carnivores*. Others are purely plant feeders, the *herbivores*, while a few tackle both plant and animal food as the opportunity presents itself, and they are called *omnivores*.

Of the carnivores, some attack and devour living prey. Many beetles belong to this group and usually their jaws are large and powerful to fit them for this mode of life. Others act as scavengers and they, or more usually their larvae, feed on animals that have died. Some carnivores, such as biting-flies and mosquitoes, are blood-suckers and have mouth-parts adapted for piercing the skin of their prey, while

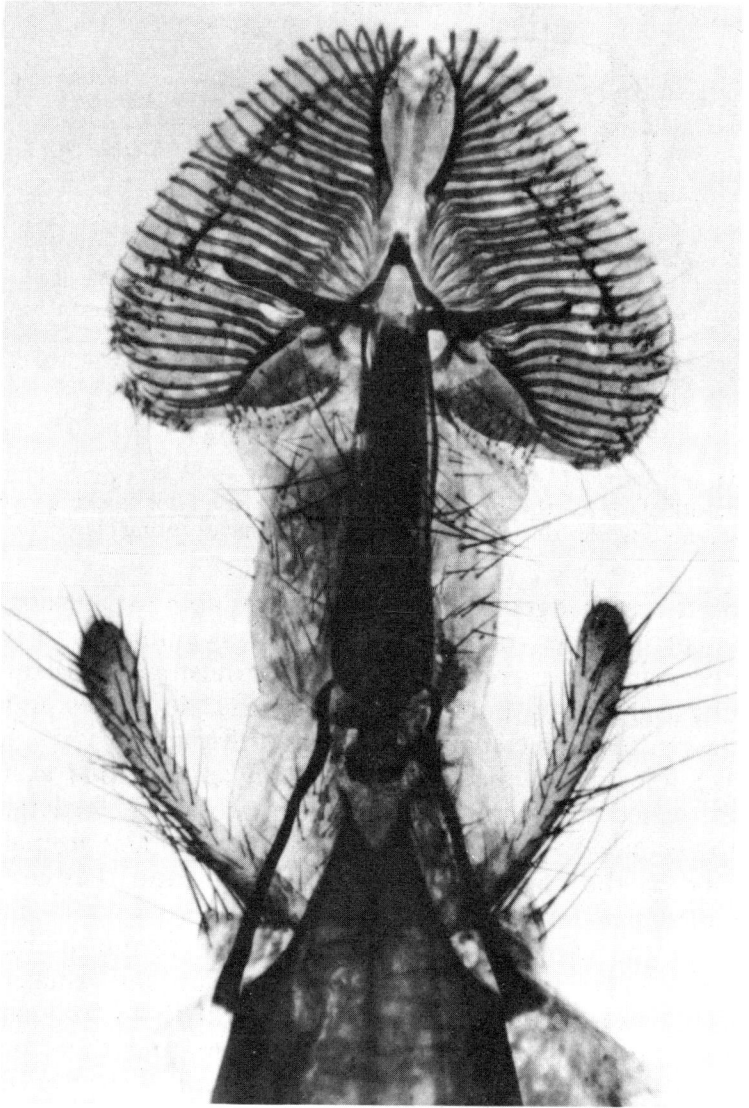

Tongue of a bluebottle fly. Liquid food is sucked up through openings in the series of fine tubes at the top of the picture. (*Highly magnified*)

there are many that are parasitic on other creatures, actually living on their hosts and devouring them or sucking their body fluids. These rather specialized insects are dealt with in Chapter 14.

Herbivorous insects feed in a variety of ways. Some devour the leaves of plants, others the bark or wood of trees. Bugs and aphids suck the sap, and bees, moths and some flies sip the nectar or take away the pollen of flowers. Perhaps the strangest method of feeding is that adopted by the gall-forming insects which by laying their eggs in a plant cause an abnormal growth to appear on the plant and thereby provide an abundant food supply for the developing larvae. Some details of these insects are given in Chapter 7.

Omnivorous insects include such domestic pests as cockroaches and houseflies and also wasps, which as well as preying on insects, also feed on fruit juices — not to mention jam.

The diet of an insect may change with the different stages of its life-history. It may be carnivorous in its larval stage and herbivorous in its adult state, or vice versa. And, of course, many insects feed only in their larval stages and not at all when they have changed to the perfect insect. Such insects as, for example, some of the mayflies do not have working mouth-parts and merely exist for, at the most, a few days to pair, lay their eggs and then die.

People often overlook the fact that moths and butterflies cannot eat solid food but can, at the most, only sip liquids. Thus the clothes-moths that are seen flying round in your bedroom are quite incapable of eating any of your clothes. It is their caterpillars that do the harm but, of course, if you do not kill the moths, they will lay their eggs in the wardrobe and so give rise to another generation of caterpillars.

6

Colouring and camouflage

I think that even those people who detest or are afraid
of insects must, in honesty, admit that many of them,
such as the butterflies, are beautifully coloured. Even
our own native insects are often strikingly beautiful
but those from tropical countries are almost breath-
taking in their magnificence. Yet gay or gaudy as their
colourings are it is often surprising how, when an
insect settles down on a plant or other support, it
merges with its surroundings so perfectly that it
virtually disappears.

Many brightly-hued butterflies have the underside
of their wings much duller in colouring. Our common
Peacock and Small Tortoiseshell butterflies are very
noticeable as they fly among our flower beds in
summer. When they alight on a flower they fold their
wings and the drab undersides of the wings become
far less noticeable. This form of protective colouring
is taken a step further in the case of the Orange-tip
butterfly in which the undersides of the wings are
mottled with green and resemble very closely the
patterning of the clusters of small flowers on umbelli-
ferous plants, such as hedge parsley, on which this
butterfly habitually settles.

Many moths have colouring and patterning on the
upper surfaces of the wings that match almost exactly

Two common butterflies and their undersides: *top* Peacock, *bottom* Small Tortoiseshell. (*Both slightly reduced*)

the bark or other parts of the trees or plants on which they usually rest. The Oak Beauty, the Peppered and Buff-tip moths are good examples and you should try to see the actual insects in your nearest museum.

Some insects have not only colour to help them to escape observation by their enemies, but shape also. This applies particularly to the caterpillars, such as those of the Early Thorn Moth, which so resemble the twigs on which they rest that it is almost impossible to locate them even though you know they are there. Among adult insects the Dead-leaf Butterflies of India are perfect examples of protective resemblances.

When we find an insect that has very bold markings, particularly if these are yellow and black, we can usually be fairly certain that it is a dangerous species

Oak Beauty Moth on and off the bark of a tree. (*Slightly reduced*)

Dead-leaf Butterfly from India. (*Slightly reduced*)

or one that birds or other creatures find is not good to eat. We ourselves draw back when we see a yellow and black insect flying near us, for our recollections of these two colours are of wasps and bees and we do not want to be stung. An example of an insect distasteful to birds is the caterpillar of the Cinnabar Moth which has brilliant and very noticeable bands of yellow and black all along its body. Such striking colours—warning colours they are called—quite the reverse of protective colours one would think, do nevertheless serve to protect their owners by advertising that they are borne by insects which are not to be trifled with. It may be said, in passing, that there are insects which appear to mimic these warning colours. Some two-winged flies, for instance, have brilliant yellow and black markings and curiously enough behave much

Owl Butterfly from South America. Hold the page upside down and you will see the resemblance to the face of an owl. (*Half size*)

as bees and wasps do when flying about and yet they cannot sting. In tropical countries there are even more striking examples of harmless insects mimicking stinging or otherwise undesirable species and thereby profiting by the deception.

A warning coloration of another kind is seen in some moths and butterflies. They have large, prominent "eye" spots on the wings and it is more than probable that any bird seeking to attack such insects would fight shy of a creature with such fearsome eyes or at least might peck at a less vulnerable part of the insect. The Owl Butterfly from tropical America not only has prominent "eyes", but its whole upper surface resembles the face of an owl and it would be a bold bird that attacked such a terrifying creature.

7

Plant galls

Sometimes when walking in the country one comes across strange growths on trees or other plants that do not seem to be normal parts of the plant. They are called galls and although not all galls are caused by insects most of them are, and the insects mainly responsible are gall-wasps—very small relations of the true wasps and bees.

A good example of a gall caused by an insect is the familiar "oak-apple", an attractive fruit-like, rose-coloured gall found full-grown at the end of May or June on oak trees. You may remember that May 29th used to be observed as "Oak-apple" Day and an oak sprig bearing an "apple" was worn to commemorate the return on that date (his birthday) of Charles II to England, and his escape after the Battle of Worcester in 1651. As the way in which this gall is produced is typical of the formation of many insect galls, it will be described in some detail.

The story really starts in the early part of the year, about January, when a tiny wingless gall-wasp might have been seen climbing from the ground up the trunk of the oak tree. When it reached the branches of the tree it picked out a nice, fat, developing bud and laid in it large numbers of eggs. At first nothing extra-ordinary seemed to have happened to the bud, but the

Oak-apple gall. (*Magnified*)

presence of the larvae which had hatched from the eggs caused the bud to swell out about the beginning of May and in a very short time it had grown into an oak-apple, at first greenish-yellow and quite soft, but by the end of May it became harder and of the lovely pinky colour of the fully developed oak-apple.

If you gathered a few of these oak-apples about June and placed them in a jar with a close-fitting lid, you would find, one day, a large number of very tiny gall-wasps, which had emerged from holes they had made in the surface of the oak-apple. Some would have wings and be able to fly but others would be unable to fly, having imperfect wings or even none at all. The flightless ones would be females. In due course these insects mate and then the females make their way down the oak trunk and enter the soil. Here they search out the small branching rootlets some distance out and lay their eggs in holes which they make in the root. Here again the presence of the larvae which hatch cause galls to grow on the roots, not oak-apples this time, but small brown swellings about half-an-inch in diameter. If you dig around the base of an oak tree about Christmas you will probably find these root

Oak-apple gall cut in two to show the larval oak gall-wasps inside

galls. From the root galls emerge in January not male and female gall-wasps as from the oak-apple, but wingless females only. They emerge from the soil, crawl up the trunk and start the whole performance again by laying eggs in the developing buds. Thus, in the life-cycle of this gall-wasp there are two generations: the male and female insects that come out of the oak-apple and the wingless females that alone emerge from the root gall. This "alternation of generations" as it is called is a very common state of affairs in oak gall-wasps.

MARBLE GALLS

A gall quite as well known as the oak-apple is the oak marble gall. It is a hard, round gall about the size of a large marble, brown in colour and very common in the countryside. Although so frequently encountered now, this gall was unknown in Britain before 1830, about which time some of the marble galls must have been brought into the country. A somewhat similar gall was at that time imported into Britain for use in dyeing cloth, and it is thought that marble galls may have been brought into the country at the same time, either by mistake or in the vain hope that they, too, would be of value for the same purpose. From these imported galls the gall-wasps must have emerged, for soon marble galls appeared in various parts of the country, spreading outward from Devon where they had been introduced. They caused something of a panic for it was thought that they would harm the trees and prevent them producing acorns, which at that time were important as food for pigs. However, there was no need for alarm as the galls do not seem to cause the mature oak trees any serious damage.

Like oak-apples, marble galls are formed in the buds of the tree, often at the tips of the twigs. Unlike the oak-apple, however, they contain only one larva and this emerges as a female gall-wasp about September or October from a neat circular hole cut in the side of the gall. It has been proved only recently (1949–50) that these gall-wasps make their way to a tree of Turkey oak, a rarer kind of oak, and cause small bud galls on this tree from which emerge male and female gall-wasps. Thus for this particular insect to survive in a district it is necessary for both kinds of oak tree to be present.

SPANGLE GALLS AND CURRANT GALLS

On the underside of oak leaves in summer there are often large numbers of small circular objects. These are spangle galls and each contains a single larva of a gall-wasp. The galls drop off the leaves in autumn and remain during winter on the ground under the tree. In spring wingless female gall-wasps emerge and climb

Two common galls caused by insects: *left* marble gall on oak; *right* Robin's Pincushion gall on wild rose

up the trunk of the tree to lay eggs on the flowers or young leaves, and from these develop larvae which cause currant-like growths—"currant galls"—to appear and become full grown about June. From these male and female gall-wasps emerge to start the cycle again.

GALLS ON OTHER PLANTS

A gall of quite a different appearance from those we have been discussing is that known as the Robin's Pincushion. It is like a tuft of bright red moss and grows on the leaves of the wild rose. It is at its best in July or August, but the gall-wasps, which may number about thirty from each gall, do not emerge as adults until the following spring.

Insects other than gall-wasps cause plant galls. One that gives rise to a very familiar gall is a saw-fly that produces the bean galls on the leaves of willow trees. From the reddish swellings on the leaves emerge larvae which pupate on the bark of the tree or in the soil nearby. The adults emerge about May and the females then lay their eggs in the leaf-buds of the tree.

Some two-winged flies—the gall-midges—also cause galls, often on smaller plants and shrubs such as nettles, bracken and meadow-sweet, although they are responsible also for galls on trees.

It has only been possible in this chapter to mention a few of the galls caused on plants by insects. Hundreds of galls are known—over fifty on the oak alone—but perhaps enough has been said to indicate a fascinating aspect of the relations of insects to plants. Moreover the study of galls is by no means complete and many facts remain to be discovered.

8

Aquatic insects

There are very few places in the world which insects have not adopted as a place to live. Strangely enough, one of these places is the sea, and only one or two species are known to tolerate salt water. The fresh-waters of the earth—rivers, streams, lakes and ponds —have, on the other hand, been invaded by hordes of insects from many different groups or orders. Some live there throughout their whole life but others spend only their earlier stages in the water. It may seem strange that creatures apparently so successful at living on land should take to a new environment, and particularly to one presenting so many problems as does water. But, of course, the adoption of water as their home has not come about suddenly but over countless thousands of years, and in that time gradual changes have come about in the make-up of the insects to fit them for life in their new abode. Undoubtedly their main reason for invading fresh water has been to exploit the immense quantities of food there, for there is a teeming life in all kinds of fresh-water habitats.

Let us consider for a moment the differences between living on land and in water. In the first place, since water is much denser than air a great deal more effort is needed to move about in it. You will know from your experiences of bathing in the sea that it is much harder to run in the water than it is on the shore. Water, too, is buoyant and quite heavy bodies are supported by the water so that they may even float.

The top of the water has a "skin" called the surface-film, which, although not differing chemically from the rest of the water, is in a peculiar state of tension and is capable of supporting objects above, or even below it. You can easily show the presence of this skin by gently laying a razor blade or a needle on the surface of water in a basin. Both objects are made of steel and as you know, steel doesn't usually float, but providing the surface-film is not penetrated, such light objects will rest on it. This layer can present problems to small creatures that live on the water for they may find it difficult to reach through it either from below or above. Most insects, however, have managed not merely to overcome the disadvantages of surface-film but actually to make use of it, as we shall see.

Among the other problems besetting a land creature that takes to the water to live is the fact that air, or oxygen, is much scarcer there than it was on land; there is only about one-twentieth as much oxygen in a given volume of water as there is in the same volume of air. Breathing, therefore, may become a problem. On the other hand the temperature of water varies less than does that of air and the changes are more gradual. This is a great advantage to small creatures for they cannot stand violent fluctuations between heat and cold. Although we might think that it was a good deal colder to live at the bottom of a pond in winter than on land, this is not so. Owing to the peculiar property of water of having its maximum density at about 39° F., any that cools below this temperature rises to the surface of a pond and freezes (at 32° F.)

48

thus forming a blanket of ice which acts as an insulator and, except in the very severest of winters, effectively prevents the rest of the water from freezing. In most ponds which are frozen over, therefore, there will be water at the bottom some degrees above freezing point in which small creatures can carry on.

Thus we see that life in water has both advantages and disadvantages, and the ways in which insects have profited from the former and overcome the latter illustrate the great versatility of these small creatures. Let us consider a few examples.

MOVING ABOUT IN WATER

If we consider any group of insects—say beetles—and compare those that live on land with those that have taken to the water we shall see some striking differences. In the first place we shall see that the bodies of the aquatic kinds are beautifully streamlined for rapid movement through the water; there are no parts sticking out that would impede the flow of water over the body and so retard the insect's movement. Looking closer we should notice that often the hind legs, which are the ones used mainly in swimming, are somewhat flattened and also fringed with long hairs, both features making them present a broader blade to the water on a swimming stroke and so making them more effective oars.

Similar features will be found on comparing land and water members of other groups of insects such as the bugs.

Thus do insects overcome the disadvantage of living in a dense medium. Some of them have even more striking modifications to their bodies for quick movement through the water. The little bluey-black beetles called Whirligigs which dart about at an incredible speed in endless circles on the surface of still waters in summer have their hind legs modified into most complicated structures. They are much flattened and comprise in effect a series of plates which can be opened and closed like a fan. On the swimming stroke they present their broad aspect to the water and give the insect an immense burst forward. On the return stroke of the leg, the plates are folded and their edges pass easily through the water with little resistance. Expert oarsmen perform a similar operation when they "feather" their oars on the return stroke.

It is surprising to find that some aquatic insects anticipated man by many millions of years in inventing jet propulsion! The nymphs of the larger dragonflies, which live at the bottom of ponds and ditches for two or three years, take in water at the tail-end of their bodies (for breathing purposes primarily) and can expel it again with such force that they are propelled rapidly through the water. This method of moving quickly proves useful when the nymphs are in danger from pursuing enemies.

Swimming leg of a Whirligig Beetle. (*Highly magnified*)

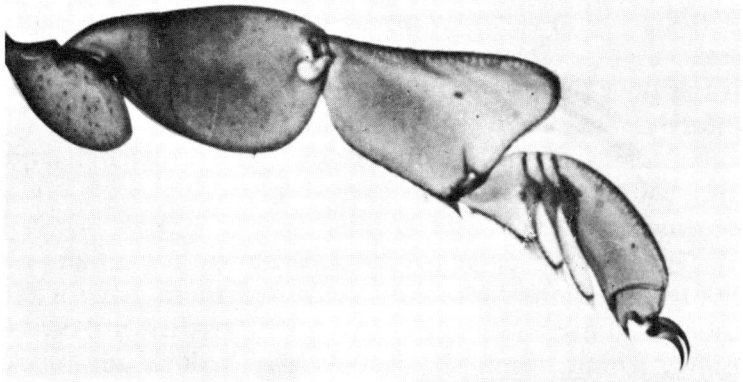

BREATHING UNDER WATER

It might be asked how we know that aquatic insects have taken to the water from the land. Could they not always have been true inhabitants of water? Well, one has only to consider the ways some of them breathe to realize that they are, in fact, in their adult stages at least, still dependent on a supply of air from the atmosphere and breathe it in the same way as do land insects (see Chapter 4), although some of them have adopted novel methods of getting their supply. This gives us grounds for believing that they have only taken to the water rather late in their development, otherwise they would surely be provided with more appropriate means of securing the essential oxygen.

A specimen of the Great Diving-beetle, a common insect in ponds and about one-and-a-quarter inches in length, will serve as a good example of one method adopted by aquatic insects in getting their air. If one of these beetles is kept in an aquarium it will be seen to rise every few minutes to the surface of the water,

Male Great Diving-beetle breathing at the surface of the water

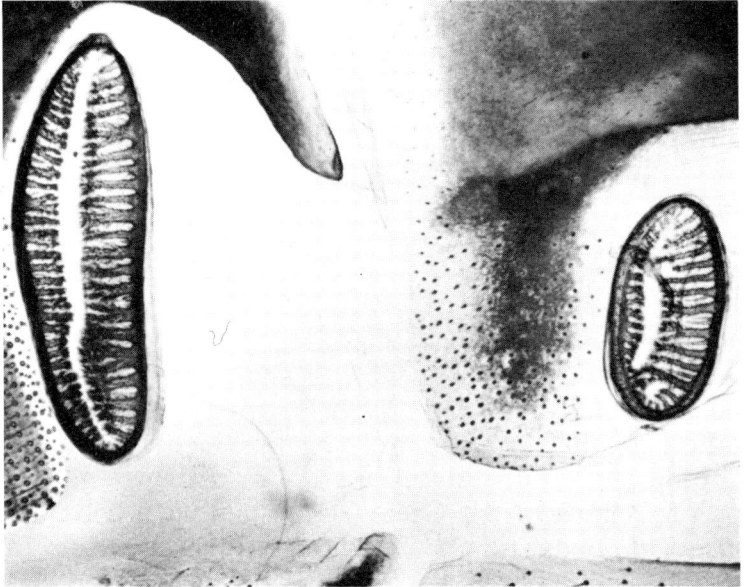

Spiracles of Great Diving-beetle showing differences in size between those at the rear of the body and the rest. (*Highly magnified*)

break the surface-film with the rear end of the body and, after resting in this position for a few seconds, descend below again. In those few seconds it has taken in air at four enlarged air-holes, or spiracles, near the rear end, but, more important, it has renewed a supply of air which it carries under its wing-cases. This supply will provide it with enough air for breathing for some minutes while it is swimming around, and then it will have to rise to the surface once more to get a new supply. Notice how the buoyancy of the water helps the beetle: as soon as the insect stops swimming it bobs up to the surface like a cork and, what is more, rear-end uppermost (because this part is the lightest part of the body) and in the correct position for taking air on board. Even a beetle that was injured could, therefore, quickly reach its vital air supply without effort.

Other aquatic insects that carry air bubbles and renew them at the surface use them in a somewhat different way. Examples of such insects are the familiar Water-boatmen which are found in ponds almost everywhere. Their air bubbles are something more than mere air reservoirs. They act as a kind of gill and as oxygen is drawn into the insects' bodies from the bubble, more oxygen passes from the surrounding *water* into the bubble and so replenishes the supply. Eventually, though, even these bubbles need renewing at the surface, and as you watch the surface of a pond in summer you will see Water-boatmen frequently rising to the surface, staying there for a short time and then diving again.

Some insects have long tubes at the rear-end of the body which they poke above the water surface when they need more air. One of these — a water-bug — is the Water-scorpion, a fairly common insect, about an inch long, found in the shallow margins of ponds. Its tube, which has no other purpose than getting air, was mistaken for a sting in days gone by and earned the insect its libellous name "scorpion".

A different kind of tube, but for the same purpose, is that of the larva of a two-winged fly called a drone-fly. Because of its long tail tube the larva has been called the Rat-tailed Maggot. It lives usually in the black mud of rather unsavoury ponds and it can make its "tail" longer or shorter to suit the depth of water.

One of the most surprising methods of breathing of any aquatic insect is that used by the larvae and pupae of some small leaf beetles. The adults are brilliantly coloured beetles that are found on waterside vegetation in summer. The females lay their eggs on

53

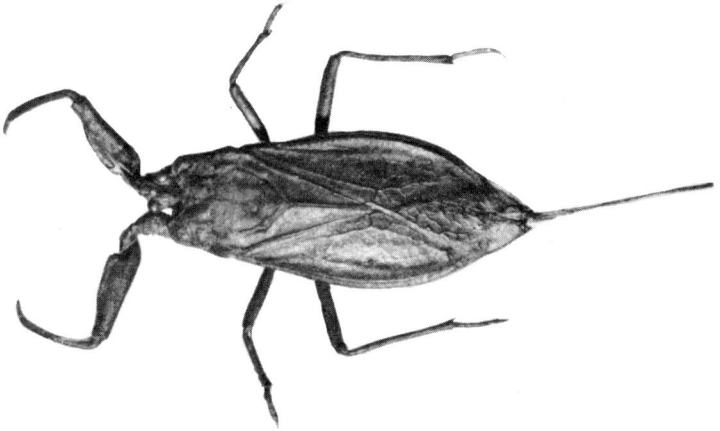

Water-scorpion: the sting-like structure at the end of the body is merely a breathing tube which can be pushed to the surface of the water. (*Magnified*)

the leaves of the plants and the young larvae, on hatching, drop to the bottom of the water. Here they search round in the mud until they encounter the root or submerged stem of a water plant such as a reed into which they bury small hollow spines on their bodies. Water plants store up quantities of oxygen for their own use and the beetle larvae (and later the pupae) tap these reserves of air with their spines and depend entirely on it while they are under water. How did they discover these air spaces in the first place and how did they become adapted to draw on them? Puzzles like this abound in the study of aquatic insects.

The larval stages of insects seem to manage their breathing problems easier than the adults. In the first place, many of them have very thin "skins" (although you will remember that these skins are still external skeletons) and there seems no doubt that oxygen from the water can diffuse through them. This is apparently the only method of breathing that many small insect larvae have. Others have flaps of this skin at various parts of their bodies forming rather simple gills, and because some of these gills have extensions of the breathing tubes in them it seems fairly clear that they are to help in getting more oxygen direct from the water. The nymphs of damselflies (small dragonflies) have such gills, but it has been found that when these have been lost the insects have still been able to live, so presumably they are only extra helps. You will remember that on page 50 I mentioned that the nymphs of the larger dragonflies take in a supply of water at their tail-end for breathing purposes. The oxygen from this is extracted by gills inside the body before the water is expelled forcibly.

The nymphs of mayflies are insects that need a lot of oxygen and they live mostly in the running water of streams which contains more of this precious gas than do the still waters of ponds. Nevertheless, to make sure that they do get enough their gills can act as paddles, and when they feel the need of more oxygen these paddles are vibrated rapidly and thereby cause water currents to flow over their bodies bringing new supplies of oxygen to be absorbed through the skin.

The pupal stages of those insects that have them also need oxygen, of course, and one pupa deserves mention on account of the way in which it manages, not only to get enough oxygen to supply its immediate needs for breathing but also to enable it to store some for a very important purpose. The pupa is that of the Black-fly, relatives of which, called Buffalo-gnats, are great pests of wild and domestic cattle in other parts of the world. The pupae can be found attached to grass stems in shallow streams and look rather like miniature ice-cream cornets in their silken cocoons. On the head of the pupa are fine thread-like gills which extract oxygen from the water. Some of this is stored as a bubble around the pupa, and when the time comes for them to emerge as adult flies they float up to the surface in this bubble, and as the bubble bursts are shot out into the air—a most ingenious method of ensuring that the delicate winged adult gets safely launched without getting wet.

Getting safely out of the water is a problem that besets many of the more fragile insects which would perish if their wings were wetted. Mosquitoes which bite us and our pets in summer have overcome this problem in a simple yet efficient way. The larvae are the familiar "wrigglers" that we find in rainwater tubs and similar places in summer. They change to pupae which are rather like outsize commas (,). These float at the surface, taking in air through a pair of "ear-trumpets", until the time for their emergence comes. Then the skin splits where it touches the

Two larvae and one pupa of the common gnat at the surface of the water. (*Magnified*)

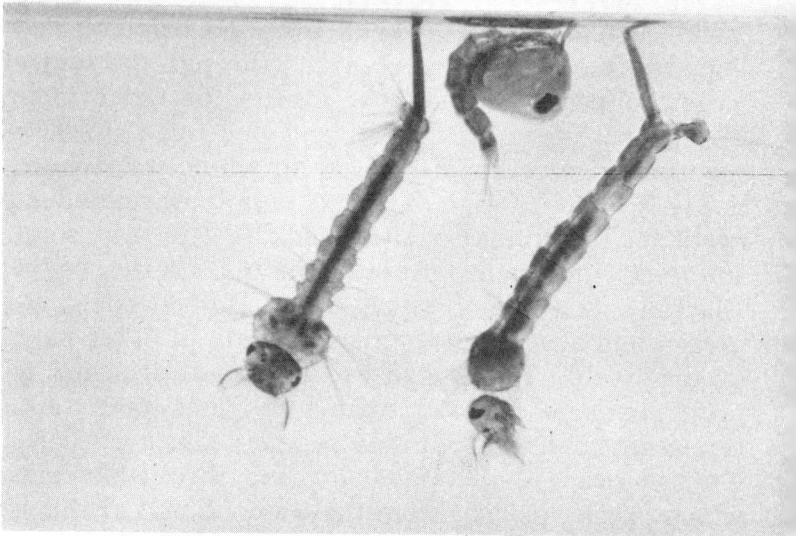

surface film, the perfect insect draws itself out of the split and rests on the old skin, using it as a raft until it is ready to fly away.

The most beautiful transformation from an aquatic stage to a winged aerial insect that it is possible to watch is that of one of the larger dragonflies. Sometimes in summer one of the rather ugly brown nymphs will be found climbing up the stem of a water plant out of the water. If one can be patient and wait for an hour or so the whole of the wonderful spectacle can be observed. First the nymph rests after its strenuous climb up the stem. Then the skin splits along the back and eventually the whole of the perfect dragonfly is drawn out laboriously through the split. The wings are, at first, mere buds, but in due course, with the pumping of liquid through their veins, they expand into the glorious gauzy wings that are the beauty of these insects. After waiting for a little time to allow its wings to harden and after a few experimental flaps the perfect dragonfly sails majestically away. Tennyson described this beautifully in his poem "The Two Voices":

"To-day I saw the dragonfly
Come from the wells where he did lie;
An inner impulse rent the veil
Of his old husk; from head to tail
Came out clear plates of sapphire mail.
He dried his wings; like gauze they grew;
Thro' crofts and pastures wet with dew
A living flash of light he flew."

HOMES UNDER WATER

Although many aquatic insects, if they are active predacious creatures, such as beetles, bugs and dragon-

57

fly nymphs, move about in the water without troubling to hide from their enemies, some of the less active kinds would soon become very tasty morsels for other creatures if they didn't have some form of protection. The larvae of caddisflies make beautiful portable cases of sticks, leaves or stones, depending on the species, into which they can withdraw completely when danger threatens. In passing, it might be mentioned that not even these cases always protect their inmates from the fierce trout who eat the larval cases and all! One kind foils them, however, for it attaches to its case long sticks which even the trout finds too big a mouthful to swallow.

Somewhat similar cases to those of caddis grubs are the flat leaf cases of the caterpillars of the China-mark Moths. These insects are unique among moths in having aquatic caterpillars and their cases are easily found in early summer on the underside of floating

Larvae of Caddisflies. (*Magnified*)

leaves—water-lily pads, and the like. The oval holes in the edges of leaves will betray the presence of the caterpillars and when the leaves are turned over the missing parts will be found with the caterpillars safely inside.

Large numbers of soft-bodied larvae do not trouble to make actual cases but merely burrow into the under-water leaves or stems of plants. When these are torn apart many wriggling "bloodworms"—the red larvae of two-winged flies (midges)—will be found in tunnels they have excavated.

INSECTS OF THE SURFACE FILM

Perhaps we might conclude this account of aquatic insects by mentioning one or two species that do not live actually in the water but on the top of it. On the

Water-cricket (*Velia*). (*Magnified*)

surface of almost any stretch of still water in summer will be seen small insects gliding, scurrying or walking across the surface film as confidently as you would across ice. They are all members of the group called Hemiptera, or bugs, and they feed mainly on the bodies of flies and other insects that have accidentally fallen on the water surface—an inexhaustible food supply. They are all light in weight and their legs are long so that what little weight they have is distributed over a wide area of water surface. In addition the legs have water-repellent properties. The effect of all these features is to ensure that the legs of the insects merely depress the surface-film into little dimples and do not penetrate it to cause the insects to sink.

The Pond-skater is the largest of these insects and as his name implies he skates across the water surface at a great rate.

The Water-measurer, a much smaller insect, extremely thin-bodied, walks very sedately, as if measuring out each stride.

The Water-crickets, more brightly-coloured than the rest, with vivid red markings, scurry fussily about in groups, keeping mainly to the edges of the pond or stream.

In this brief survey of some of the insects that have adopted water as their home we have seen, perhaps better than can be seen in any other type of habitat, the wonderful way in which insects have become adapted to live successfully in environments which might seem at first sight completely unsuitable to them. They have not merely overcome the disadvantages of the new surroundings but have turned them to their own advantage and this is typical of these very adaptable creatures.

9

Insects and our crops

As we saw in Chapter 1, insects form the largest group of the Animal Kingdom, far outnumbering both in kinds and individuals all other animals put together. They also reproduce at an alarming rate and, if they had no enemies, they would soon multiply in numbers to such an extent that they would destroy all the plant life on the earth's surface. All animals are ultimately dependent on plants, for even if they are not themselves vegetarians, they eat those that are, and thus all animal life throughout the world, including man and insects as well, would be wiped out.

Happily for us, insects *have* many enemies. They provide the food, wholly or in part, of a great number of birds, mammals and other creatures and of course they attack each other. Ladybird beetles for instance keep down the populations of "greenfly" on our crops; ichneumons are parasites that kill off a great number of insects; and dragonflies catch and eat many kinds.

Nevertheless, there are still more than enough insects left to cause man to regard them as his most serious rivals and enemies and in this chapter we are going to consider a few of these harmful kinds. Many of them are our enemies because they eat or destroy the plants that we ourselves need for food. There is scarcely a crop that we grow that is not attacked by some insect or other. Some eat the leaves and thus prevent the plants from making their own food so that they die or are stunted. Some attack the flowers and prevent the fruit from developing, while others eat the fruit itself. Plant-bugs suck juices from the plant stem or leaves and may, at the same time, introduce a disease. Feeding first on a diseased plant they suck up with its juices some of the disease-producing substance—a virus—and then introduce it into the next healthy plant that they visit. Our potatoes suffer severely from such virus diseases spread by plant bugs.

The roots of plants are attacked by many insects, mostly in their larval stages. The large grubs of crane-flies, or "daddy-long-legs", called "leather-jackets" are great pests of our farm crops such as mangolds, potatoes and grasses. But probably the most serious pests of this kind are the creatures called wireworms—the larvae of click-beetles—which normally feed on the roots of grasses. When grassland is ploughed up so that other crops can be grown, the wireworms attack these, particularly if they are corn crops. During the last war, when it was vital to grow as much corn as possible, and much old grassland was ploughed up to do so, wireworms became one of our greatest problems, and the government had to employ many entomologists to try and circumvent the pest.

Even our large forest trees are seriously attacked by insects and now that large-scale forestry has grown into such an important industry it has become a vital part of the forester's work to keep these particular insect pests in check. One of the worst of our native species is the beautiful little green moth called the Green Oak-roller, whose caterpillars in some seasons strip all the leaves off oak trees over a very wide area in southern England. Although they do not kill the trees, they make the trees grow more slowly and reduce the value of the timber taken annually from a wood.

Some beetles tunnel under the bark of trees to reach the food materials made by the plant. Sometimes, when the bark of a fallen tree is stripped off, the tunnels, often radiating in all directions where the beetles have been working, can be seen. In the case of the Elm-bark Beetle, one of our worst pests of this kind, the female cuts out a small tunnel and then after pairing, lays her eggs in holes at the side of it. When the larvae hatch they cut out side passages for themselves, resulting in the characteristic pattern of radiating tunnels. Naturally, these tunnels do a good deal of harm to the tree. (See drawing below.)

Anyone who has fruit trees in his garden will know only too well of the large number of insect pests that try to deprive us of our crops of apples, pears or plums. Perhaps the best known, because it is so

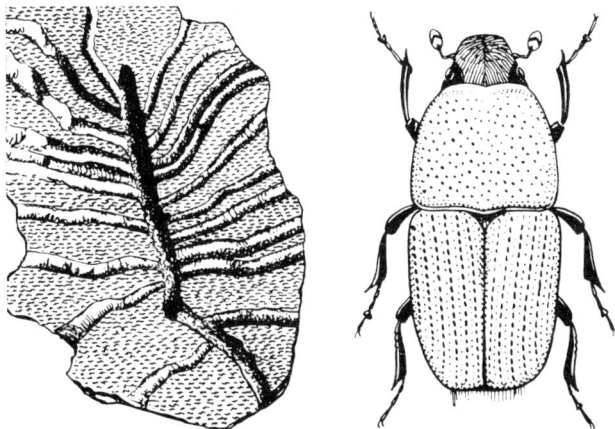

The Elm-bark Beetle with *left* a sample of its tunnels under the bark of a tree. (*Insect magnified*)

easily seen, is the American Blight, or Woolly Aphis, which attacks apple trees. The white tufts of what look like cotton-wool are the protective material surrounding a colony of plant-bugs or aphids. Apart from the injury and disfigurement caused to the apple trees by the aphids themselves, a fungus disease, called Apple-canker Fungus, gains entry into the wood of the tree through the wounds caused by the Woolly Aphis.

Even when our crops or timber have been safely gathered and stored, they are still attacked by insect pests. A whole host of small beetles, moths and other insects are a constant menace to those who have control of warehouses, stores, shops or even houses where food products are stored. A special department of the Ministry of Agriculture, Fisheries and Food, with a large staff of scientists, exists to give advice to such people in the identification and control of these insects. Neither is our furniture or the structure of our houses and other buildings safe from insect pests, for wood-boring beetles of several kinds, including the Death-watch Beetle, mentioned on page 31, do immense damage by excavating tunnels as they feed. The one most frequently seen in houses is a small beetle about a quarter-of-an-inch in length, the females of which lay their eggs in crevices and cracks in floors, doors or furniture. The resulting larvae—woodworms —tunnel into the wood, often remaining there for several years before emerging as adult beetles. The small round holes that we notice on our woodwork are the exit holes where the adult Furniture-beetles emerged.

All the insects we have considered in this chapter so far have been British, and although they cause trouble enough indeed, we must consider ourselves fortunate, for in other countries the damage done by insects is on a much larger scale, as we shall see later. This is particularly so in regions of the world where immense areas are given over to the cultivation of one particular crop. In the United States, for instance, vast acreages are devoted to the growing of cotton and an insect called the Cotton-boll Weevil—a kind of beetle—has at times been responsible for the destruction of half the American cotton crops, worth millions of pounds. This perhaps gives us a clue to the way in which any particular insect becomes a pest. It does so only because man has brought about artificial conditions which have favoured its rapid increase. Most insect pests were, until recently, quite harmless insects which fed upon some particular food and their numbers were controlled because there was only sufficient of it to support a limited population. As soon as man began to cultivate particular plants for his own use in large quantities—cotton, wheat, potatoes—he immediately provided large supplies not only for himself but also for the insects that normally fed on them. With plenty of food available, they had one limiting factor on their increase removed and they multiplied out of all proportion to their previous rate. The Colorado Beetle was originally a harmless insect feeding on the leaves of wild plants of the potato family in the Rocky Mountains of North America. It was not until the early American settlers spread westwards and grew their potato crops in the area in which it lived that it became troublesome, and now since it has spread to Europe (but not, happily, to Britain) it has become one of the worst pests of potato growers.

Some insects, too, have become troublesome because they have been introduced accidentally, perhaps on their food plants, into places where their natural enemies are absent and they are able to multiply rapidly as a consequence.

LOCUSTS

The insects which are individually man's greatest enemies in his role as food producer are, however, locusts. Locusts are a kind of grasshopper, and there are at least seven different kinds which rank as major pests. They are no new enemy of man and the eighth plague of ancient Egypt mentioned in the Bible was a plague of locusts. It is difficult for us in Britain to get any idea of what a swarm of locusts is like and it must be seen to be believed. There may be so many flying locusts in a swarm that a shadow resembling the darkness of night may be cast on the ground at noon and continue for hours. In a single swarm the insects may weigh several *thousand tons*. When they settle after their flight they cover everything and when they move on not a green living thing is left. For centuries these vast hordes of insects have ravaged huge areas of land from the west coast of Africa to India and from the Caspian Sea in the north to Tanzania in the south. They have arrived without warning, no one knew from where, left a whole country devastated and caused the death by famine of their populations. At the present time, even though a good deal of knowledge is being gained about the insects, their ravages are estimated to cost mankind an average of £15,000,000 annually. What is worse they have frustrated man's attempts to produce more food in those tropical countries now being opened up and developed, where it is so vital.

During the last thirty years intensive research by

entomologists has added greatly to our knowledge of locusts and has made possible measures to control them which are now being put into operation. The first approach made was to find out details of the life-history of locusts and it was astounding that although these insects have been such major pests of man for centuries, it is only in recent years that some of the more important of these details have been discovered. The female locusts lay their eggs in the ground, usually in packets of between thirty and a hundred. The nymphs which emerge resemble their parents except in size and in the absence of wings and are called "hoppers". Although they may gather into parties at this stage they do no particular harm but lead their independent lives. Under certain conditions, however, related to the overcrowding of large numbers in a restricted area, they become restless, develop longer wings than they would normally have, become bigger and change their colour. So different are these locusts in the *gregarious phase* from the normal solitary individuals, that they were, until quite recently, believed to be a different species. With the development of this phase, the migratory instinct comes about and suddenly they will take to wing to wreak havoc on crops many miles from their place of birth and often, indeed, in another country. This fact alone has proved one of the biggest obstacles in the control of locusts. When the damage is outside their territory, it has been difficult to persuade governments to take steps to eradicate the insects; and once a plague has passed, even the country that has suffered has often been loath to provide the large amount of money needed to prevent a recurrence.

Now, however, the problem is tackled on an international basis for at least two of the locusts that do most damage—the Red Locust, which lives in East and South Africa, and the African Migratory Locust of West Africa. An Anti-Locust Research Centre in London receives reports from the locust areas by the quickest methods, often by radio, and can thus forecast accurately where swarms are likely to occur so that information can be sent to the areas concerned and measures prepared in advance to combat the locusts or to destroy them before they start on their way.

The methods of attack include the spraying of poisons from aeroplanes on to roosting or flying swarms, the draining of areas of country to make them unsuitable as breeding grounds for locusts and killing off the insects in the "hopper" stage so that swarming is prevented.

The problem is so vast and the areas of the world which are involved are so extensive that it will be many years before man has successfully conquered his old enemy, the locust.

10

Insects and disease

Although the damage caused by insects eating our crops is serious enough, the most dangerous of our insect pests are those that carry disease, either to human beings or their domestic animals. Happily, in Britain now, very little serious illness is caused by insects although, as we shall see later, this was not always so. Our domestic animals, however, are still plagued by a few troublesome insects.

In tropical countries several very severe diseases are insect-borne and the culprits in most cases are various kinds of mosquitoes—two-winged flies related to the gnats that are such nuisances to us in summer. The mosquitoes, it must be stressed, are perfectly harmless insects in themselves. The males are never troublesome for they live merely by drinking plant juices. The females of the different kinds of mosquitoes suck the blood of man or animals because it is an important food for them in aiding in the development of their eggs, although even for that purpose it is not essential as it was once thought to be. The trouble from mosquito bites arises from the fact that the insect's method of feeding lends itself to the passing of disease-causing "germs" from an infected human being to a new victim.

If there are plenty of infected people in a particular

locality, there is a very good chance of a female mosquito sucking the blood of one of them and then flying to another victim, sucking his blood and so passing the disease on.

If, on the other hand, sufferers from the disease are absent, there is no chance of contracting the disease. In this country, for instance, there are plenty of the kind of mosquitoes that can spread malaria, one of the most serious insect-borne diseases of mankind. However, as malaria is now an extremely rare disease in Britain, the bites of the mosquitoes, although they may be painful, are otherwise quite harmless.

In warmer countries than ours, malarias of various kinds remain among the greatest afflictions of mankind. In the past they have killed more men than wars have ever done, have wiped out whole armies, decimated cities and may have been the major cause of the downfall of the Greek and Roman civilizations. Our own country has not escaped the ravages of malaria, for as "ague" or "marsh-fever" it was a very common and serious illness until about a century ago, particularly in marshy districts such as the fens of Lincoln and Cambridge and along the banks of the Thames. The name of the disease is derived from the Italian words, *mala aria*, meaning "bad air" because it was for centuries believed damp marsh air was the cause of malaria. However, we know now that minute single-celled organisms which can only be seen with a powerful microscope are responsible and that these are passed from infected to healthy people by various kinds of mosquitoes. The relation between the disease and damp, marshy places is simply that such areas are the breeding haunts of mosquitoes and now that much of our fenland and marshes has been drained, the disease has almost disappeared in this country.

The mouth-parts of the female mosquito are in the form of boring and sucking organs and when she drives them into a blood vessel she also pumps in at the same time a salivary fluid which stops the blood clotting. If the blood is that of a sufferer from malaria some of the malaria parasites are also sucked up and, if they are in the right stage, continue their development in the blood of the insect, passing eventually from its food canal into its salivary glands. While this development is going on, the mosquito can bite people without causing the disease, but as soon as the malaria parasite has reached the stage of its development when it is in the salivary glands, the mosquito, in pumping out the salivary fluid into a new victim, also pumps out the parasites and so infects him.

The discovery of the mosquito's part in transmitting malaria was made in 1898 by a British Army officer in India, Major (later Sir) Ronald Ross, and he undoubtedly ranks as one of the greatest benefactors of mankind. His researches were carried out under great difficulties and involved an immense amount of patient work, including hundreds of minute dissections of mosquitoes to unravel the complex life-history of the malaria parasite. Once he had proved to the world that the disease was insect-borne, the way was open to wipe it out, firstly by protecting people from mosquito bites and secondly by attacking the insects at the most vulnerable stage of their life-history. It is fortunate that mosquitoes become active only as night approaches so that ordinary daytime activities of human beings are not affected by the control measures. At dusk, however, the covering of exposed parts of the skin and the erection of mosquito-proof screens across windows and doors of dwellings effectively prevented the insects gaining access to new victims.

The destruction of the insects was made fairly easy by the fact that the larvae, although living under water, must breathe atmospheric air and rise to the surface to take it in through their breathing-tubes. On large stretches of water, therefore, which it was impracticable to drain completely, all that was necessary to do was to spray oil over the surface. Being lighter than water it spread as a fine film across the surface-film and effectively prevented the mosquito larvae from getting air and thus killed them off. Poison, too, can be sprayed on to the water.

The adoption of such measures and, of course, the use of drugs which kill off the malaria parasite if it has managed to enter the human blood stream, have wiped out malaria in many areas of the world where it was once rife, and made them safe for human habitation. Nevertheless, there are still vast stretches of land where either through the ignorance of the inhabitants or other causes, malaria still takes a heavy toll of human beings.

YELLOW FEVER

Yellow fever is another dreadful disease of tropical countries that is similarly carried from man to man by a mosquito, but of a different kind, and has plagued man for centuries. It afflicted the early Aztecs of South America, caused enormous mortalities among the followers of Christopher Columbus and spread from South America along trade routes, first to Central America, the Southern United States and then to the West Coast of Africa. The causes of the disease were thought to be such varied factors as droughts and floods, mangrove swamps, high temperatures and so on.

When it was realized that the disease was spread by a particular kind of mosquito, steps were taken to try and wipe out the disease in different areas. Of several large-scale attempts, perhaps the most dramatic was that carried out during the building of the Panama Canal which joins the Atlantic to the Pacific Oceans. The first attempt to build the canal in 1880–89 had failed partly because of the immense death-rate from yellow fever and malaria among the workers. For the second attempt the American Sanitary Department in 1904 organized a campaign under the control of General Gorgas to make the canal zone—a strip of land about ten miles wide by forty-five miles long—healthy and habitable. War was declared on the yellow fever mosquito and also the malaria mosquito.

All the breeding places of the insects were destroyed; even bottles and old cans in which water might collect were cleaned up. Ditches within a hundred yards of any dwelling were drained, and rank grass, in which the adult mosquitoes might rest during the day, was burned. Any breeding places that could not be drained were treated with oil and anyone who left an open vessel of any kind holding water near his dwelling was fined. Over 1,200 men were employed on the work, with inspectors in charge of each district to see the work was carried out in a thorough manner. The result amply justified the effort for in the next year (1905) not a single case of yellow fever occurred in the area and this happy state of affairs continued afterwards.

Without the patient studies which entomologists had carried out on the malaria and yellow fever mosquitoes, their life-histories, structure and habits, long before it was known that they were of such importance, the human race might still be ravaged by these dreadful diseases.

SLEEPING SICKNESS

Another killing disease of the tropics that is carried by insects is sleeping sickness in man, and the equivalent disease in cattle, nagana. Victims contracting these diseases become at first lethargic, then paralysed and finally pass into a coma and die. For hundreds of years the diseases have been known to exist on the coast of West Africa, but as the African continent was opened up for trade, sleeping sickness spread right across and made whole regions uninhabitable.

In 1903 it was discovered that the organism causing these two diseases was spread from victim to victim by two-winged flies called tsetse flies. They belong to the same order as our common houseflies and are a little larger than they are. Unlike houseflies, however, they are biting insects and it is when sucking the blood of a victim that they introduce into his blood stream the parasite causing the disease.

Tsetse fly

Man and his domestic animals are not the only creatures in which the parasites can live. Most of the wild animals for which Africa is famous harbour them and, strangely enough, are apparently unharmed by them. They act, however, as a gigantic reservoir of the disease and it is only necessary for a tsetse fly to bite one of these wild animals, pass to a human being or domestic animal, and so transmit sleeping sickness or nagana.

Sleeping sickness is an immense problem to those who are planning the development of Africa and may never be solved. There are twenty-two different kinds

74

of tsetse flies and they have varying requirements of food and places to live. Methods which are successful in destroying one kind may not be suitable for destroying others. It has been suggested that big game should be slaughtered wholesale, or driven far away from all possible areas occupied by human beings or domestic animals in the hope that the tsetse flies will be deprived of this immense store of parasites and may eventually become harmless. The Southern Rhodesian Government did, in fact, carry out this policy between 1932 and 1940 and slaughtered 30,000 wild animals yearly in an attempt to eradicate the disease from their country. And although, even today, a certain amount of restriction of game is carried out in many parts of Africa, attempts are being made to establish reserves away from human settlements where the game can live in peace. Nevertheless, these measures can at best be only temporary, for man presses further and further into Africa to exploit its immense resources. New drugs and new techniques in insect control seem to offer the greatest hope of, at least, alleviating this immense problem.

THE HOUSEFLY

A dangerous, but usually overlooked pest that is constantly in our midst in summer is the housefly. It cannot pierce our skin to inject disease-producing germs but achieves much the same purpose in a far more insidious way—by poisoning our food. Houseflies feed by sucking up liquid food of all kinds and in their search for it love to wallow in all kinds of filth and garbage—manure heaps and the like. Their legs and tongues become covered with many kinds of germs and when they fly on to our food they transfer these germs to it. Even worse, they frequently suck up far more food than they can eat, and when they settle on something even more attractive, they vomit up part of the previous meal! Thus it comes about that houseflies carry diseases of many kinds. The most serious of these is typhoid and before their disgusting habits were realized, they caused immense losses in human life. It was said that in the Spanish-American war of 1898 more soldiers were killed by typhoid than by bullets, about eighty per cent of the total deaths being due to typhoid. Similar losses took place in the Boer War and there is little doubt that the disease was spread by houseflies, some of it being carried from infected filth on the bodies of the flies, some in the digestive organs of the insects.

"Summer diarrhoea" among infants is another disease that is carried by houseflies and as recently as 1911 about 2,000 died of this in London alone.

However, greater cleanliness in towns, the covering of dustbins and the reduction of manure-heaps, where the insects breed as well as feed, has greatly reduced the numbers of houseflies in our time and correspondingly the amount of fly-carried disease.

And so one could go on mentioning more and more diseases both of man and animals for the carrying of which insects are responsible. It is now known that over 250 such diseases are so carried. Gradually their severity is being overcome by advances in medical knowledge, but particularly by close study of the insects responsible, so that they can be controlled at their most vulnerable stages. Who, reading even this very brief account, can doubt the value to mankind of the study of insects which has been and is being made by generations of entomologists or "bug hunters"?

11

Some beneficial insects

In this chapter it will be a relief to turn from insect enemies to a consideration of some insects that are distinctly beneficial to man.

The first in this category to come to the minds of most people is undoubtedly the Honey-bee which has been a benefactor of mankind since prehistoric times. A painting from the later Old Stone Age found in a cave in Eastern Spain shows a woman collecting honey from a wild bees' nest, and ever since those early times, and in many parts of the world, man has ruthlessly plundered the honey which bees have stored away to tide them over the unproductive winter months. With bee-keeping today such a well-practised art, where every endeavour is made to preserve the bees and take only the honey surplus to their requirements, it may seem strange to us to remember that it was not until about 100 years ago that a type of hive was invented from which it was possible to remove the honey without harming the bees. Before then, and, it must be confessed, even for long after that time, bee-keepers destroyed the colonies of bees in order to take their reserves of honey, whether they were wild stocks or kept in hives.

Although the production of honey is the feature of bees that first comes to mind, there is another and vastly more important function that they perform for us: the fertilization of many of our crops, particularly of fruit, by carrying pollen from one flower to another. The gardener, fruit-grower and nurseryman are dependent on bees for this very necessary operation. It is true that other insects, for example some butter-flies and moths, as well as beetles, also help in this work of pollination, but their activities are on a much smaller scale than those of bees, they are less depend-able and what is more, those insects often give rise to hordes of devouring larvae which destroy the plants their parents fertilize.

Bees, however, are completely under control, do not harm the crops they pollinate, can be increased in number in any locality merely by setting up hives and ensure the fertilization of most of our cultivated plants

A modern type of beehive which has movable frames on which the bees can make their waxen comb

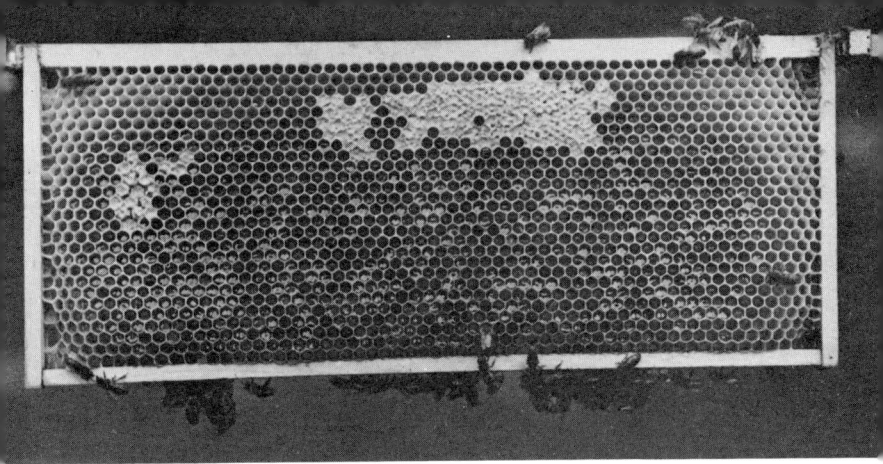

A single frame removed from the hive showing honeycomb; the cells which have a capping of wax are full

that are not wind pollinated (as are, for instance, the cereal crops such as wheat and oats).

Both hive-bees and wild humble-bees are fitted for gathering and transferring pollen from almost every type of flower. Other insects, including the wild solitary bees, such as mason and leaf-cutter bees, can only tackle a restricted range of flower types.

A fuller account of bees and their relatives is given in the next chapter.

THE SILKWORM MOTHS

Another insect which man has domesticated for his own benefit is the Silkworm—the larva of an insignificant white moth which must originally have been a wild species in China. Legend has it that silkworms were known in that country 2,000 years B.C. Although there are one or two other caterpillars that produce a commercially usable silk, the finest silk in the world is still obtained from the cocoons of this original species. For centuries the methods of silk culture remained a closely-guarded secret held only by the

Chinese, but in the sixth century A.D. two Persian monks who had been missionaries in China brought knowledge of the industry to Europe and later they smuggled out some silkworm eggs in bamboo canes. The production of silk was started first in Constantinople; by the twelfth century it had spread over Europe and, with government encouragement, had become particularly active in France and Italy, in which countries it has remained an important industry. Several attempts were made to produce silk in Britain but they failed. However some years ago Lady Hart Dyke, after studying the methods of the Italian silk rearers, began silk production in a small way at her home, Lullingstone Castle, near Eynsford in Kent and later at Shenley in Hertfordshire. Commercial silk rearers feed their silkworms on the leaves of white mulberry and although, when need be, silkworms will feed on black mulberry, or even on lettuce, they will not produce good silk on these foods. When the silkworms are full grown they spin their cocoon in which to pupate and it is, of course, the covering of this cocoon which is the pure silk of commerce. It is produced by the silkworms as a sticky liquid which issues from a pair of tube-like glands opening by two minute holes on the underside of the mouth. As soon as the liquid oozes out of the pores and comes into contact with the air it hardens and the two streams unite to make a single thread.

In a silkworm factory, a proportion of the cocoons are set aside so that the moths may develop normally to give a breeding stock to perpetuate their kind. The rest of the cocoons are put into warm water or in steam which kills the pupae within and also softens the gum which covers the silk. Then the ends of the silk are caught up by girls and attached to reels which

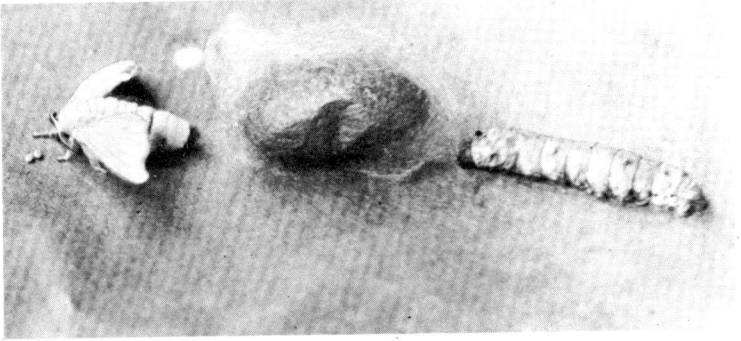

Life-history of the silkworm moth; two eggs, the moth, the silken cocoon and the caterpillar or silkworm

wind off the silk. Each cocoon yields about 300 yards of silk and the strands from a number of cocoons are reeled together to give the raw silk of commerce. The outer silk of the cocoons is unsuitable for reeling and is kept separate for other purposes.

As a result of long domestication the moths which are allowed to emerge from the cocoons have lost the power of flight and can only flutter their wings uselessly. After pairing, the females lay their eggs on the paper lining of the box and shortly afterwards both male and female moths die without having taken any food. The eggs are stored in a cool place until early next summer as it is important that they should not hatch until supplies of mulberry leaves are on the trees.

SCALE-INSECTS

Two other insects which have been exploited commercially by man are the Lac Insect and the Cochineal Insect. They both belong to a group of true bugs called "scale-insects" so named because the bodies

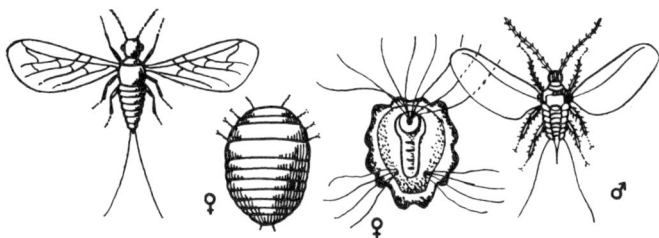

Two insects useful to man: the Cochineal Insect *left*, and *right* the Lac Insect. The female insects, from which the commercial products are obtained, are the ones without wings. Note how their bodies have become changed in shape compared with the normal males in each case

of the females, particularly, become covered with waxy scales formed of a substance they exude from their rear end.

They feed on the sap of certain plants and a great deal of sap must be sucked up to provide them with enough of the materials they need for food. The waste part of the sap, changed now in composition, is given out by the insects and when it comes into contact with the air hardens into a waxy material.

The Lac Insect is a native of India and crowds in such numbers on the twigs of certain trees that the waxy scales—the lac—form a continuous layer over considerable areas. The twigs are gathered and pressed between rollers to separate the lac from the wood and after melting and washing it is sold in sheets as shell-lac, better known to us as shellac, an important material in the manufacture of varnishes and polishes for wood and metal, ink used in lithographic printing, sealing wax, gramophone records and many electrical products. The sediment from the water in which the lac is washed is pressed into cakes of crimson lake— used in the manufacture of the paint of that name and formerly of great importance in the dyeing industry. The introduction of synthetic dyes made from coal tar has, however, made crimson lake of minor importance as a dye, as it has also cochineal—a similar product exuded by the Cochineal Insect, a native of Mexico which has been introduced into the Canary Islands and at several places on the shores of the Mediterranean.

Formerly cochineal was an important red dye and a valuable export of countries producing it, but now it is hard to think of any use to which it is put except, perhaps, the decoration of fancy cakes!

EDIBLE INSECTS

Perhaps this last use of insects—as a dye for red, fancy cakes—has come as a surprise and perhaps a shock to some readers. But insects of some kinds have provided large parts of the diets of human beings from time immemorial—and continue to do so in some parts of the world even today.

Were not the Israelites in the Bible urged by Moses to eat locusts, beetles and grasshoppers? Even in our time locusts are highly esteemed as food in parts of Africa, Arabia and Iran where they can be bought in the market places as everyday items of commerce. The "Red Indians" of North America also ate locusts.

Crickets, the caterpillars of certain moths, ants, termites, beetles, water-bugs and the larvae and pupae of bees are also insects that have at some time, and by some people, been considered delicacies.

12

The social insects:
Bees and Wasps

The term "social insects" includes those insects that
have taken to living in colonies consisting perhaps of
thousands of individuals. Although some form of
social life is seen in other insects, it is in four groups
—ants, bees, wasps and termites or "white ants"—
that it has proceeded to its greatest development. It
will be noticed that the first three of the groups—ants,
bees and wasps—are all members of the order Hymenoptera. The termites, in spite of their popular name
"white ants", are not in any way related to the other
social insects. They belong to the order Isoptera and
are, in fact, much closer related to the cockroaches than
to the true ants.

Social life began among insects millions of years
before it did with man. Fossils of ants which lived
30,000,000 years ago have been found which show
that they were then just the same as they are today,
and even in those far-distant days were differentiated
into the social castes on which the organization of a
colony depends today. It is believed that in the world
generally there are close on 10,000 species that live
in more or less social conditions and in Britain we
have seventy social insects.

If we think of a human community—a city for
instance—we can see that for it to work successfully

Worker

Queen

Drone

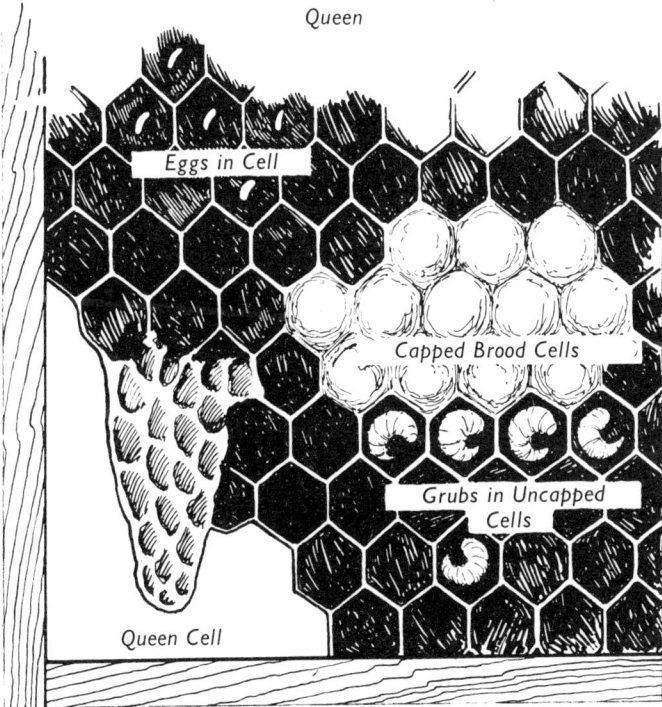

The Honey-bee: the three castes and a portion of the broodcomb in a hive. Note the differences in size and shape between the queen, worker and drone

there must be people performing different tasks. Whereas in earliest times, before man took to living in groups, every family had to do everything for itself —catch the food, make clothes, protect itself and so on—once he had hit on the idea of living with his fellows it no longer became necessary for *everyone* to do *everything*. One man could catch the animal food, another could make the clothes, others could guard the community and so on. This division of labour is the basis of a social community and by freeing men of the necessity of doing everything for themselves enables everyone to have a fuller life with more leisure for doing the things they want to do. Since man adopted this way of living perhaps 10,000 years ago, it has enabled him to become civilized and given him opportunities for developing the intellectual part of his being.

With the social insects, too, this specialization of certain individuals for particular tasks has brought about similar advantages in providing abundant food for large numbers, in tiding over the winter and in protecting the insects from their enemies. The great difference between their social life and ours is that it has not enabled them to develop their intellect although, as we shall see, it has resulted in the unfolding of remarkable examples of instinctive behaviour.

In the communities, or colonies, of all the insects which have developed the most advanced social life, three distinct types of individuals are found: a "queen" who is a fully developed female and whose function is to lay all the eggs in the colony; a male or males to fertilize the queen; and large numbers of infertile or undeveloped females who carry out all the work of the colony. Let us see how this works out in a colony of honey-bees in a hive. In a strong "stock" of bees, there may be up to 80,000 undeveloped females or "workers", some 400 males or "drones" and a single "queen". Soon after the queen hatched she left the hive on a mating flight, followed by the drones and, after pairing, she returned to the hive perhaps never to leave it again until she dies. Her life-work consists of laying single eggs in each cell made by the workers. In the course of her useful life of three years she may lay as many as 1,500,000 eggs at the rate of two a minute or 3,000 per day during the season.

The eggs take about three days to hatch and the young larvae are cared for by the workers. At first they are all fed on "royal jelly", a secretion produced by glands in the heads of the workers. A few may continue on this diet in which case they, too, will develop into queen bees. Most, however, have a change of food after a few days and receive pollen and honey. These larvae, after pupating, develop into either drones or workers, depending on whether the egg from which they hatched was fertilized or not. It is believed that the queen bee can control the sex of the egg as she lays it by holding back or releasing the male sperm she has received and which she has stored in a special sperm-containing vessel in her body. The cells in which drones develop are larger than those containing worker grubs and the queen-cells are bigger still and hang downwards.

Soon after emerging from the pupal stage, the workers begin their life of toil. They do all the work of the colony, beginning perhaps by cleaning the hive and feeding the larvae of their own kind as well as those of drones and queen, graduating through duties such as guarding the entrance from possible enemies, ventilating the hive by "fanning" their wings vigorously, manufacturing wax and building with it the combs which serve as larders for the store of honey and pollen or as cradles for the young. Later they will become foragers, searching out in the adjoining countryside supplies of pollen, nectar and water. The pollen is gathered on the hairy body of the worker as it goes from flower to flower, and we saw in Chapter 11 how important this part of the bees' activity is for the fertilization of our crops.

The pollen grains are combed out of the hairs with a special series of stiff bristles on the hind leg and then transferred to a hollow, fringed portion further up the leg which is called the pollen basket. In this way the load of pollen is made more convenient to carry back to the hive.

Propolis is a gummy substance gathered by the bees from various trees and, like the pollen, is carried back to the hive on their back legs. It is used by them for filling up cracks in the hive to exclude draughts or to make it water-tight.

Nectar, the sweet liquid obtained from flowers, is sucked up by the workers' hollow tongue which is longer than that of either the queen or drone. It is converted into honey in the honey sac of the worker, the cane sugar of the nectar being changed into the grape sugar of honey by its mixture with the secretion of certain glands in the insect. The honey can be disgorged into the cells of the hive when it is intended to store it or the bee can open the mouth of the stomach just below the honey sac if she wishes to feed herself.

A word, perhaps, may be said in passing about wax, the material of which bees' cells are made. It is a natural secretion of the worker bees only and is produced in a liquid state by glands in the body and moulded by wax pockets on the underside of the abdomen into little scales. The bees whose part it is to manufacture the wax form clusters in the hive, remaining in this state for hours and so, by increasing the temperature in the mass, facilitate the production of the wax. As the clear scales of wax appear they are taken into the mouth to be made flexible and are then transferred to other workers to be fashioned into the cells of the hive. The shape of the cells in a bee-comb is a wonderful example of a structure which combines both strength and capacity with the minimum expenditure of material and labour. Its hexagonal or six-sided shape is, of course, a result of building numbers of cells in contact, and no other design would give such support for the adjoining cells and provide as much space within with such a small amount of material.

The life-cycle of the hive begins in the early spring when, with the returning warmth of the sun, the queen stirs and, passing from cell to cell, lays in each a single egg. The workers whose function it is to be nurse bees tend each larva as it hatches, feeding it until it is ready to pupate and then sealing the end of its cell. The clusters of bees always milling around the cells provide the warmth necessary for the development of the young. As the population of the hive increases in this way, more combs of cells are built by other workers and still others assiduously collect the pollen, nectar and water with which to feed the many hungry mouths. As supplies increase much is stored in combs which are also sealed with wax caps.

It may happen in the early summer that conditions in the hive become too congested and then the bees "swarm". Filling themselves with what honey they can carry, many of the workers, together with the queen, leave the hive in a cloud and collect on an adjoining bush or tree in a great mass. If not taken by a bee-keeper they will eventually fly off and settle in a distant tree or house and there start another home.

Before they set forth on their swarming flight the workers will have constructed several large queen cells and now in these the bees remaining in the hive will be rearing larvae to become queens by feeding them on "royal jelly". The first of these to hatch searches out all the other queen cells and kills off their occupants with her sting. Shortly afterwards she sets out on her mating flight and, returning to the hive, assumes the position of her predecessor.

With the approach of autumn and the decrease of the supply of nectar being brought into the hive, it becomes important to conserve the stocks stored up in the honeycomb so that the colony will have enough food for the winter months. And so at this time, the drones, who are performing no useful purpose in the hive, are either killed off or driven away. The days shorten, the weather becomes colder; gradually the queen ceases to lay and the workers collect on the centre combs of the hive clustering together for warmth until spring returns once more to awaken the hive to activity.

When they are collecting food from flowers, bees often fly distances of a mile or more from the hive. By careful experiments, a German scientist has been able to show not only that the bees on their return to the hive are able to tell their fellows of a supply of nectar that is available, but also how far away it is *and in what direction.* So accurately can the returning foragers impart this information that the other workers are able to go to the exact spot, even if it is as much as three miles away! The experiments by which Professor Karl von Frisch discovered this amazing ability of bees are described in the book by him, mentioned in the Book List, and make fascinating reading. Briefly it can be said here that he found that the returning foragers carried out little dances on the comb and the type of dance—for instance, whether it is a "round dance" or a "tail-wagging dance", indicates to the surrounding bees the distance of the food supply. Further, the direction in which the dances were performed, gave the direction in which the food lay.

A "round dance" indicates to the surrounding bees that there is a plentiful supply of food near to the hive. The dancing bee, on returning to the hive, turns around in a circular movement first to the right, then to the left, repeating these movements again and again for half a minute or longer at the same spot. Then she may move to another part of the honeycomb and repeat the performance.

The "tail-wagging" is carried out in a different manner. The bee runs a short distance in a straight line, wagging her abdomen about from side to side rapidly. Then she makes a turn through a complete circle to the left, runs straight ahead once more and turns a circle to the right. The dance is repeated over and over again and experiments have shown that it indicates to the other bees a supply of food some considerable distance from the hive. The number of turns in the dance and the rate of turning tell the actual distance.

The bees witnessing the dances become greatly excited and follow her, keeping their antennae close to her body, possibly to detect the scent she has carried from the particular flower she has been visiting. Then first one, then others, turn away, leave the hive and search out the food supply so wonderfully described to them.

Perhaps the most striking aspect of the dances is their ability to indicate the direction in which the food lies. When the bees are dancing on a horizontal surface the direction of their dance points towards the source of food, but when as often happens, they dance on the vertical combs in a hive they can still indicate to their fellow workers the right direction, and this direction seems to bear relation to the direction of the sun. Bees, apparently, are able to ascertain the sun's position even when the sky is cloudy and the clue to understanding why this is so is believed to lie in the construction of their wonderful compound eyes.

The communal activities of the hive bee in building up a great store of honey during the summer, on which the whole colony can survive in an active state throughout the winter, is unique among insects. It is a feature which, by making the insects worthwhile for man to "cultivate" for his own ends, has led to their distribution over the whole world. It is believed that originally hive bees must have been native to Asia and although today there are many races or varieties of honey-bees which are characteristic of different countries or areas, they all belong to this same species, *Apis mellifica*.

There are, however, social bees truly native to our own country such as the bumble-bees which are common insects of our gardens. The big clumsy bodies of some of them and their noisy hum as they fly from flower to flower are familiar sights and sounds in summer. Many people believe bumble-bees cannot sting. They can, and do sting but not so readily as hive bees. There are nineteen species of true bumble-bees in Britain and again their colonies include the three kinds of individuals—queens, workers and drones. Unlike hive bees, however, all except the queen die off in the winter. About March or April the queens search out suitable places in which to build their nests. These may be in small tunnels or holes left by field-mice or other animals and are made of grass, leaves or moss. Into the nest the queen bumble-bee collects food in the form of a paste of pollen and honey and on this she builds a large wax cell in which to deposit a number of eggs. After sealing this over she makes another large cell—a "honey-pot"—really to contain the honey that she has gathered.

The bees which eventually develop from the eggs are all workers and they now take over the foraging and storage of food, building of cells and protection of

Door lock containing cells of a Mason Bee

the nest, the queen remaining at home to lay eggs. At its peak a colony of humble-bees may include 400 bees so that it is very much smaller than that of a hive bee.

Towards the end of the season the queen lays eggs, some of which develop into male bees and others into queens. After mating, the young queens leave the vicinity of the nest and, in due course, search out nooks and crannies where they can spend the winter in a state of hibernation; the drones and workers all die off in the autumn.

Not all our native bees are social; the great majority, in fact, are solitary insects, working only for themselves. Such are the Leaf-cutting Bees which cut neat shapes out of the edges of rose leaves with which to make their tubular cells. Others are the Mason Bees, which form cells from particles of earth, small stones, etc., cemented together with a salivary secretion. One of these insects frequently chooses for its home a lock of a door in a garden, filling it with its cells and using the keyhole as a convenient entrance.

WASPS

There are nearly 300 different kinds of wasps in Britain alone, but to most people the word "wasp" brings to mind the large yellow and black insects which frequent our gardens and which become such nuisances in late summer when they come in great numbers into our houses and feed on jam or fruit. There are six common kinds of these large wasps and they are all social insects. Some of them build up large colonies during the summer, but unlike the hive bees they do not store up food with which to survive the winter, and only the queens live through until the spring.

With the first warmth of early spring the queen wasps, which are larger than the workers or males, are seen on the wing, eagerly searching out suitable places in which to make their nest. Some species of wasps choose a cavity in the ground, but others make nests in trees and occasionally in houses or outbuildings. Wasps do not make their nests of wax, but of paper which they manufacture from wood rasped off with their powerful jaws from trees, gateposts or palings and then chewed up until it forms a paste. Layers of this pulp are spread on the roof of the cavity chosen by the queen for her nest and in due course she builds her comb of cells, all opening downwards, with an umbrella-shaped covering above the comb. In each cell an egg is laid and, to prevent it from falling out, is glued in. From these eggs develop workers and once these have appeared the queen wasp devotes herself to egg-laying, leaving the workers to collect food, care for the young larvae and build more combs of cells. These are added in tiers joined on to each other by pillars. At the end of the summer there may be as many as seven or eight combs and the nest may be much bigger than a football.

The larvae are fed on other insects and, during the summer, wasps are useful creatures because they destroy immense numbers of garden pests. The adult wasps partly chew the food before giving it to the larvae and receive in return a sugary saliva from them. Wasps take about five weeks to complete their development from egg to adult. Towards the end of summer the workers build larger cells than normal and these are used to rear queens which alone will survive the winter and give rise to new colonies next spring. Males, too, appear at this time to fertilize the young queens. Male wasps, like male or "drone" bees, have no stings,

95

since these structures are in reality a modified form of egg-laying apparatus. Males differ from the ordinary worker wasps also by having longer antennae.

The pretty nests made by the tree-wasps are usually found in autumn when the leaves have fallen and they are, of course, deserted by then as the occupants have died off. A much larger nest sometimes made in buildings, but more typically in hollow trees, is that of our giant wasp, the Hornet, which is quite common in parts of southern England. Although it looks such a fearsome insect, it need really cause no alarm for it is much less prone to sting than the commoner wasps. Of course, when it does sting, it makes a good job of it! Apart from its larger size, the hornet can be distinguished from the other wasps by the bands on the body which are not black like theirs but brown. The yellow coloration of the hornet is also of a deeper shade.

A small wasp's nest with parts of the side cut away to show the tiers of cells in which the larvae are reared. The opening of these cells is at the bottom. (*Reduced*)

13

The social insects:
Ants and Termites

Although the social life of bees and wasps is, indeed, wonderfully organized, it is among the ants that we see this way of living carried to its highest development. All ants—and there are over 3,000 species in the world—are social insects, although some kinds have only small colonies consisting of perhaps a dozen individuals to a nest; on the other hand, other kinds may have up to half a million individuals in a single colony.

Ants are nearly all small insects, although the Giant Ant of the Amazon region of South America is about three-and-a-half inches long; often, however, they have long lives. Some queens are known to live for over fifteen years and workers up to seven years. They are, too, much less restricted in their diets than are bees and wasps, and their investigations into our own larders and store-cupboards make some of the species rather troublesome.

The nests of ants are nearly always underground, and usually consist of a somewhat irregular series of chambers and passages excavated in the soil, in contrast to the orderly arrangement of cells in a beehive or wasp's nest. This trait is, however, not a disadvantage to the ants for it lends itself to much freer behaviour without the limitations of making

97

their homes always to a set pattern and, if conditions become unfavourable, it is a simple matter to construct a new nest elsewhere in a short time.

The young ants are not reared in special cells but are carried from chamber to chamber as they develop, and it seems important to them to have rather exact conditions of humidity and temperature at each stage. The worker ants tend the young most assiduously, constantly licking them and carrying them about. They are fed sometimes on food regurgitated by the workers from their own crops, or on solid food placed in their mouths, depending on the species of ant, and, as with wasps, the workers receive back some secretion from the larvae which serves as food. The larvae change into pupae in about eight days and in some species the pupae are enclosed in a cocoon. The "ants' eggs" sold by pet shops for feeding goldfish and birds are, in fact, the cocoons of the Wood Ant, one of our largest species which lives in wooded areas.

After the pupal stage, lasting about two weeks, the adult ants emerge and these take the usual form of social insects—workers, males and queens. In some colonies, too, there may be "soldiers" which are large workers with extra large heads. Occasionally, too, by some freak of nature, there are individuals which seem to partake of the characteristics of two forms; they may be part male and part worker or part worker and part queen.

Only the males and queens are winged and on a day in July or August, usually when the weather is warm and humid, they leave the nest on a wedding flight. It is a spectacular occasion and ants seem to be everywhere; birds are quick to take advantage of the opportunity of such an abundance of food. It seems as if the exact weather conditions are necessary before the flight can take place, for, down in the nests, the workers will forcibly restrain the males and queens from setting forth if conditions are unsuitable.

It should be mentioned, in passing, that a mating flight does not take place in some species; in the Wood Ant, for instance, pairing takes place on the ground.

After mating, each queen returns to earth and proceeds to lose her wings. She rubs them against objects on the ground and finishes off the job by biting them off. Immediately the self-mutilation has taken place the queen's sole idea is to find some place underground into which to go. She may return to the nest she left but probably more often takes up her residence in another nest or starts a completely new nest of her own by making a cavity in the soil. The first larvae which hatch from the eggs she lays must, of course, be fed and tended by her, but when they have developed into workers they take over the duties of the nest, leaving the queen free to lay eggs, and feed her on liquid food which they regurgitate.

A single nest may have several queens in it, for, unlike queen bees, ant queens are not hostile to members of their own sex. Thus a colony may grow to huge proportions and perhaps branch out into a number of neighbouring colonies. This is not to say, however, that all ants are friendly to one another. The ants of separate colonies, even if they are of the same species, may be very hostile to one another, and when ants meet there is a great deal of stroking each other with antennae and in that way no doubt the "nest smell" of friends or the absence of it in enemies is ascertained.

Queen and worker ants, by the way, can sting and although they do not hurt us as much as bees or wasps, the stings of a lot of ants, when, perhaps, we have by mistake sat on one of their nests, can be painful enough. The poison is not the same in all ants, but in the large Wood Ant it is formic acid which has been used for many medicinal purposes and even for flavouring the icing of cakes!

BRITISH ANTS

In Britain we have twenty-seven different kinds of ants and one of the commonest is the Common Black Ant, a small black species, abundant in gardens.

Perhaps the most interesting features of these ants are their large-scale dairying activities. Many ants are fond of the sweet liquid called honey-dew which is exuded at the rear end of plant-bugs, such as green-fly. The Common Black Ants "farm" these insects by making enclosures, surrounded by earth walls, in which to keep them. These "pastures" are often to be seen at the base of leaves on which the plant-bugs themselves feed, and sometimes the bugs are sheltered in chambers within the nest. The ants lick up the honey-dew as it exudes from the plant-bugs and they help the process by stroking the body of the insects with their antennae.

The Common Yellow Ant is another species that farms plant-bugs and even cares for the eggs of these insects throughout the winter. When the larvae of the bugs hatch in the spring the ants carry them out of the nest and place them on their correct food-plant. The nests of the Yellow Ant are usually in open places such as fields or on hills. They are long in shape and higher at one end than the other. An interesting feature of these nests is that they lie in an east-west direction, the highest part of the mound, in which the ants live, being towards the east. In the hilly districts on the

Continent, where this ant is also very common, this property of the nest has been of value to walkers and climbers in pointing out the direction to take when they have been lost.

In woods, particularly pine woods, a large mound, up to three or four feet high, may often be seen. This indicates the presence of Wood Ants, our largest British species. The actual nest of the ants is well below the mound, the latter serving only as a place where the ants can enjoy the sun's warmth and where they may bring their larvae for warmth in summer. The mounds may persist for a great many years and the colonies may grow to huge proportions. Since

Section of Nest

Female   Worker   Male

Wood Ants and a section of their nest at the base of a pine tree these ants feed largely on other insects it will be seen how valuable they are for keeping down insect pests; it has been estimated that a hundred thousand insects may be killed in a day by a colony of Wood Ants and as a consequence, in Germany, they are protected by law.

In examining the colonies of Wood Ants it is as well to bear in mind that when disturbed these insects can squirt their poison—formic acid—from glands at the rear end of their body for a distance of over six inches and the tiny droplets on the skin can cause great irritation.

Ants' nests are remarkable for the number of guests they shelter. No less than 300 different kinds of creatures, mostly insects but also some mites and threadworms, have been recorded from the nests of British ants alone. Some are mere scavengers for, although ants are extremely clean and tidy insects, inevitably a certain amount of debris collects in a large colony and, perhaps because they are such scrupulously clean insects themselves, the ants seem to tolerate these scavengers, which include beetles and some fly larvae.

Other guests are more than tolerated, they are welcomed and even fed and looked after by the ants. These include the larvae of certain beetles, and the secret of the welcome they receive is that they, like the plant-bugs, produce secretions that the ants lick up eagerly. In the case of one kind of larva, they are so fond of the secretion, that the ants even overlook the fact that the beetle larvae devour their own grubs!

Another "guest" is the caterpillar of the Large Blue Butterfly which similarly exudes a secretion enjoyed by the ants. The caterpillar at first lives a free existence, feeding on wild thyme, but eventually leaves this plant and wanders about until it meets a Red Ant. After a time this seizes the caterpillar in its jaws and carries it back to its nest, when it immediately sets about devouring the ants' offspring! Nevertheless, in all fairness, it should be said that it does give in return the liquid which the ants so eagerly desire. In due course the caterpillar pupates in the nest and eventually the beautiful Large Blue butterfly crawls out of its subterranean chamber into the open air. This life-history is undergone by all Large Blue butterflies and presumably if a caterpillar does not meet with a Red Ant at the right stage of its development it dies. For years the mystery of what happened to the caterpillars of Large Blue butterflies remained unsolved, and little wonder. It was not until 1915 that the patient investigations of two well-known entomologists, F. W. Frohawk and E. B. Purefoy, eventually found out the secret.

Some occupants of the nests can scarcely be called guests for that term implies some degree of toleration on the part of the host. These include various ichneumon flies which are parasitic on the ants or their young and eventually bring about their death.

Ants, too, like human beings, are not free from robbers. There are Robber Ants which make raids on the peaceable nests of other ants and carry off pupae to their own colonies. There is nothing haphazard about these raids; they are organized in the same manner as a human war. Scouts are sent forth to spy out the territory and particularly to find out where lies the best chance of attack. The main force then sallies forth and if the battle goes against them they send reinforcements. The pupae captured are not devoured; they are reared in the nest of their captors and used as worker-slaves when they emerge as adults.

ANTS IN OTHER COUNTRIES

In Britain ants hardly cause us much concern. As we have seen, they occasionally invade our pantries and become minor nuisances but, generally speaking, their social life rarely impinges on ours. It is not so, however, in other countries and in the tropics some kinds of ants are among the greatest afflictions man can have.

Take, for instance, the Driver Ants of tropical America and Africa. They make no permanent nests but march about in tremendous colonies. Guided by their acute sense of smell (for they are almost blind), they scour the jungle, devouring anything in their path, even killing animals of the size of horses and cattle if tethered and unable to escape their terrible jaws. Barriers such as small streams are crossed by the ants forming living bridges of their own individuals. If a human dwelling has the misfortune to be in the path of an army of these dreaded creatures there is nothing to be done but evacuate it until, having explored every nook and cranny of it and devoured everything edible within, they have passed on their relentless way.

We have seen that some British ants have, at least, become dairy farmers. The technique of agriculture has been taken a great deal further by some foreign ants. Solomon, you may remember, gave this advice to lazy people: "Go to the ant, thou sluggard; consider her ways, and be wise: which having no guide, overseer, or ruler, provideth her meat in the summer, and gathereth her food in the harvest." (Proverbs, Chapter VI, verses 6–8.) It is believed that Solomon had in mind one of the Harvesting Ants which are remarkable farmers. They live in the desert or semi-desert regions where long periods of drought make both plant and animal life scarce. They gather the seeds of plants, carefully remove the seed coverings, carrying away this "chaff" and drying the grains in the upper parts of their nests, and then store them where they are not likely to get wet. If heavy rains do reach their store they carry the seeds out for drying in the sun. Some of them clear areas around their nest and, on these bare patches, seeds which have been accidentally dropped sprout into new grasses and this has given rise to the belief that the ants actually sow their crops.

The Leaf-cutter Ants, which are common in Texas and the south-west of the United States generally, do grow their own crops—of fungi which serves as the food both for the adults and developing larvae.

The fungus is cultivated intentionally by the ants in special chambers in their nests set aside for it. When the young queens leave the nests in which they were born they eat heartily of the fungus supply in the nest and carry some with them on their wedding flight in a little pocket which all ants have in the front of their mouths. When they set about preparing for a nest of their own in the usual way they eject the fungus from the pocket on to the floor and it starts to grow. They tend it with care, manuring it with their own excrement and even breaking up some of their own eggs to provide growth substances needed by the fungus. When eventually workers develop from the first eggs the queens have laid, they take over the culture of the fungus along with their other duties. As the crop of fungus grows, more "compost" is needed on which to cultivate it, and now the workers go out in long processions to neighbouring trees and cut off pieces of the leaves, carrying them back to the nest over their bodies like banners. The leaf fragments are packed into the special underground chambers and left to decay. Other workers, smaller than the foragers, spend their whole lives in these fungus chambers, keeping the leaves wet with their own excrement. Eventually, the mass becomes suitable for growing the fungus, which appears as white threads, studded with clusters of small spherical swellings. It is the latter that are bitten off and used as the staple food for both young and old.

That this technique of growing the fungus is not accidental is shown by the great care the ants display in regulating the ventilation of the "fungus gardens" by opening or closing some of the numerous holes leading to the outside air, and in drying their pieces of leaves at the entrance to the nest if they have become wet with rain. In some way, too, the ants seem to have the ability to control the kind of growth which appears on the fungus threads. When the particular kind of fungus is grown in a laboratory the small white heads do not appear, and, once the ants have abandoned a nest, a large fruiting mushroom structure appears on the fungal threads which never occurs when the ants are in residence.

We have seen how fond ants are of the substance honey-dew, a sweet secretion they obtain from plant-bugs. Sometimes honey-dew is found on plants where these bugs have been and is a favourite food of ants. A sweet liquid like this is not easy to store up for the winter and ants have not learned the secret possessed by bees of storing up sweet liquid as honey, in cells in their nests.

However, one group of ants, the Honey-pot Ants, which live in dry regions of the south-west United States, have found an almost equally successful way of storing honey-dew to tide them over the dry season. Certain workers of each colony become living "honey-pots", taking in all the honey-dew that is brought in by foraging workers and storing it in their bodies. Of course, after a few weeks their abdomens become tremendously swollen and they become quite incapable of walking, so they hang from the roof of a chamber in the nest, clinging on by their claws, When their fellows need food they stroke the "honey-pots" who then regurgitate their honey-dew a little at a time. This is a remarkably successful way of preserving a perishable food supply.

TERMITES

As we saw earlier, termites or "white ants" are not related to ants but belong to a much more primitive group of insects. Nevertheless their behaviour so closely resembles that of ants that they can conveniently be considered in this chapter.

Termites are among the most abundant insects in the tropics and they all live in colonies. There are some differences, however, in the castes as compared with other social insects and there are only three stages in their life-history—egg, nymph, adult instead of the four in ants, bees and wasps.

In the first place, there are both male and female workers in about equal numbers in a typical colony. They are white, have no wings and are blind. Then there is a caste of "soldiers" both male and female, whose main function is the defence of the colony. They too, are wingless, have huge jaws and heads, the latter protected with hard "armour". Finally, there is a "king" as well as a "queen" in each colony and the pair live together in the nest.

The king and queen are winged and they alone seem able to face the light of day, the other castes

107

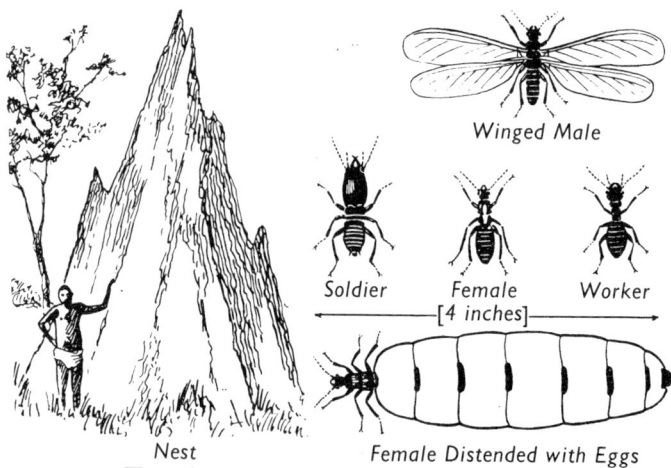

Winged Male

Soldier   Female   Worker
    [4 inches]

Female Distended with Eggs

Nest

Termites and their huge nest-mound

remaining always away from the light. They go on one flight, not this time a wedding flight, but a dispersal flight to establish a new colony. Having arrived at their chosen spot, they descend to the earth, lose their wings and pair. Once the queen has set about in earnest her life task of laying eggs she becomes an incredible size—over four inches long and rather like a white sausage.

Although some kinds of termites live in nests which remain underground, the larger and better-known termites erect huge structures above the original nest formed by the queen. These may be as high as twenty feet and are made of earth or partly-digested wood cemented with saliva. They are so strong as to be almost indestructible with anything less powerful than dynamite!

There is no entrance above the ground to these huge, towering edifices, as termites shun light. From the nest, however, lead underground tunnels, often many yards in length and spreading in all directions, along which the foragers travel in search of the wood

108

or other plant material on which they feed. Their fondness for wood makes them the great pests of man that they are, for no wooden structure is safe when termites are in the neighbourhood. Their habit of working away from light also means that they attack wooden structures from the inside and their tunnels can be considered extensions of those leading from the nest. They reduce the interior of wooden objects—walls, floor-boards, furniture—so thoroughly that they leave only a thin, paper-like shell on the outside, and their activities are not realized until some pressure on the damaged timber suddenly makes it collapse!

Not only domestic timbers are damaged by termites, of course; telegraph-poles, railway sleepers, wooden bridges, landing stages and fences are all attacked and this damage is serious, not only on account of the monetary value of the property lost but because it may endanger human life. Books too, since they consist largely of wood fibres, are rapidly devoured, which means that valuable libraries in the tropics must be built on termite-proof foundations.

Strangely enough, termites cannot themselves digest the wood which forms their food. They rely on certain single-celled animals, or *Protozoa*, in their food canals to break down the cellulose in the wood by special ferments into a form that can be used by the insects. As in ants, the food is regurgitated and there is a good deal of interchange of food between various castes in the colony.

Some termites cultivate fungi in a similar manner to that adopted by the Leaf-cutter Ants, a remarkable example of a useful habit being discovered independently by two widely-differing groups of insects.

Can any good be said of termites? Their only value

seems to be in breaking down the large quantities of rotten wood which would otherwise accumulate in the tropics, and we mustn't forget that, as we saw in Chapter 11, native tribes find termites a desirable part of their diet.

Here we must leave the subject of social insects. There is a great temptation, in considering the wonderful way of life that some of them have adopted, to compare their social life with ours. But we must be quite clear in our minds that their behaviour, incredible as it may be, is not as a result of a high development of reasoning intelligence as it is with us.

The colonies are kept together by reason of having a common food supply in one place. The food store, by providing nourishment at a time of year when it cannot be gathered in the ordinary way, enables the insects to survive over bad periods instead of dying and thus builds up large communities.

The care for the young may have originated as nothing more than a search for food, for we have seen that the larvae frequently provide nourishment for those feeding them and some are also often covered with oily secretions of which the adults are very fond.

Cultivation of fungi, pasturing of "ant-cows" and all the other startling developments of social life may all have started as unorganized, perhaps accidental, searches for food. In the course of time—and this may run into millions of years—these methods have become built into the behaviour of the insects as instincts. It is in this light, as instinctive behaviour, remarkable but blind and purely automatic, that we must regard the organization of insects into societies.

14

Parasitic insects

The word "parasite" always has a somewhat unpleasant sound as it indicates a creature that lives at the expense of another. In the world of natural history there are many living things, both plant and animal, that have adopted this form of existence.

Naturally, insects having tried out most ways of living, have adopted this one too and some insects are among the most successful parasites.

Entomologists give a somewhat special meaning to the word parasite, when applied to insects. A true parasite sucks the blood or otherwise feeds on the body of another animal (called the "host") but rarely kills it.

The host in such a case is almost always much larger than the parasite as, for instance, a bird, dog or human being.

On the other hand there are some insects that, in their larval stages, feed on other insects and bring about their death. To these the name "parasitoid" is given.

True parasites include such creatures as fleas, lice and bed-bugs and it is these, perhaps more than any others, that have been responsible for building up in people's minds such unpleasant associations when the word "insect" is mentioned.

FLEAS

Fleas occur on most warm-blooded animals and usually each animal has its own particular kind of flea. Cat-fleas and dog-fleas do, however, occasionally attack man and conversely the flea that is particularly attached to man is sometimes found on cats and dogs. Fleas only stay on their host for part of the time and live elsewhere, as for instance in a dog's bedding or a bird's nest, when not feeding on their host. When a flea sucks the blood of its host it injects at the same time a secretion which slows down the clotting of the blood and it is this which sets up the irritation of a "flea-bite".

There are about a thousand different kinds of fleas in the world and in the course of time, as a result of their way of life, they have all become modified in form in a most remarkable manner. They have lost the wings they once had; their bodies have become flattened from side to side to enable them to travel easily through the fur or feathers on the host's body; and their legs have become developed into powerful jumping structures, a feature which no doubt helps them to reach their large hosts—and also enable them to escape quickly too!

Although fleas are now only a minor pest to us, and then only where large numbers of people are crowded together in unclean surroundings, in other parts of the world today, as they were in our own country long ago, they are serious menaces to health. One species that normally lives on rats, but which also attacks man, carries the disease of bubonic plague—the Black Death—which devastated even Britain in times gone by and which still wipes out huge populations in other countries.

LICE

Lice are of two kinds; biting lice and sucking lice. Biting lice have mouth-parts fitted for biting and they are mostly parasites on birds, feeding on pieces of feather or scurf from the birds' bodies.

Sucking lice have mouth-parts specially adapted for piercing skin and sucking blood and they live more or less permanently on their hosts. Three kinds of these are parasites of man: the Head-louse; the Body-louse and the Crab-louse. When people are crowded together with infrequent opportunities of changing clothes, as in war-time, infestation by lice becomes common and, quite apart from the discomfort caused by the parasites sucking the victim's blood, lice can transmit dangerous diseases such as typhus and trench fever.

THE BED-BUG

The Bed-bug is a true bug belonging to the order Hemiptera, but like all parasitic insects has become greatly modified, particularly by losing its wings and having a greatly flattened body which enables it to creep into the narrow crevices, cracks and joints in a bedroom in which bed-bugs spend their time during the day and in which they lay their eggs. At night they emerge from their hiding places and attack human beings in bed, piercing the skin with their "beak" and sucking the blood. They also feed readily on other animals. Like most sucking insects, the bed-bug can transmit disease from one patient to another.

PARASITOIDS

The insects which attack others of their own kind and

113

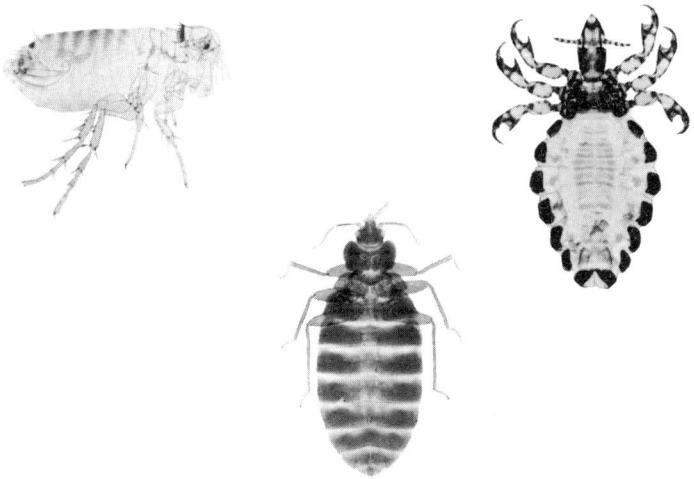

Three unpleasant parasites: *from left to right,* human-flea, bed-bug, louse from a pig. (*All magnified*)

eventually bring about their death, all belong to two groups—the two-winged flies, or Diptera, and the group to which ants, bees and wasps belong, Hymenoptera.

The largest and most striking are those that belong to the former group and they go under the general name of tachinid flies. There are a great many species, but the general appearance is that of an ordinary housefly, except that they are usually more brightly coloured. Their life-histories are, however, quite different from that insect. Some lay their eggs on the bodies of the host they have selected and when the larvae hatch they burrow into its body, feeding on its internal organs and so bring about its death, but not until the larvae have completed their development.

They pupate in the host's body or bore their way

out and pupate in the ground. Others lay their eggs on the food of their hosts and the young larvae get eaten and so gain access to the hosts' bodies. In some species the female actually lays her egg inside the body of the host or maybe introduces a larva which has already hatched. Perhaps the most extraordinary method adopted is that where eggs are laid in places frequented by the hosts and the young larvae merely sit upright on their "tails" waving their bodies about in the hope of making contact with a host. This is, of course, rather a "hit-and-miss" method and so, to make up for the many larvae which will not find a host, the female fly lays a great many eggs.

The hosts of tachinid flies include practically all kinds of insects and also woodlice, spiders, centipedes, worms, snails and birds. Caterpillars are favourite choices as are beetles and plant-bugs. Some tachinids attack many different kinds of hosts, whereas others keep more or less to a few or even to one host.

It seems incredible that insects which have adopted a parasitic mode of life should themselves be hosts for parasites, yet such is the case. Some of the second group of parasitoids belonging to the order Hymenoptera, mentioned on page 17, attack the larvae of the tachinid flies. Some flies, too, which are normally parasitic on caterpillars, will when the chance presents itself transfer their attentions to any tachinid larvae which are also in the body of the caterpillar, so that the unfortunate creature carries within it a parasite within a parasite! How true is the old rhyme:

> Big fleas have little fleas
> Upon their backs to bite 'em.
> Little fleas have lesser fleas
> And so *ad infinitum*.

The hymenopterous kinds of parasitoids belong to two types: ichneumon flies and chalcid-wasps. They are nearly all very small insects and some of the chalcid-wasps include perhaps the smallest insects in the world, mere specks only one-fiftieth of an inch in length, even in the adult stage.

Evidence of ichneumon flies is often seen on caterpillars in the garden. The caterpillar of the Large or Cabbage White butterfly, if examined carefully, will sometimes be seen to have attached to its dead body a number of small yellow egg-like objects. These are the cocoons of one of the commonest ichneumon flies, the female of which laid her eggs under the skin of the caterpillar. The larval ichneumons feed on the fat body of the caterpillar, carefully avoiding eating any of its vital organs. When they are fully developed they gnaw their way out of the skin and spin their yellow cocoons on the caterpillar's body. At this stage the caterpillar dies, just when it would normally be pupating; the activities of the parasitoids have gradually sapped its life away, but not until they have completed their own development.

Ichneumon flies are important agents in keeping down the numbers of caterpillars and kill off many that would do harm to our crops, although, of course, they attack also insects which do no damage.

Even if a Cabbage White caterpillar escapes the attentions of an ichneumon fly it is not out of the wood yet, for now a chalcid-wasp may attack it in the pupal stage. It is said that the wasp may even settle down near a caterpillar that is about to pupate and wait until the event has taken place. Then she pierces it with her egg-laying apparatus and places a supply of eggs inside the body. The larvae emerging from these kill off the pupa.

116

Not all parasitoids have such an easy job to find their hosts so that they can lay eggs in or on it. There is a large ichneumon fly, *Rhyssa*, about one-and-a-quarter inches long—a most exceptional size for an ichneumon fly, which, as I said before, are generally very small insects—that lives in British woods and

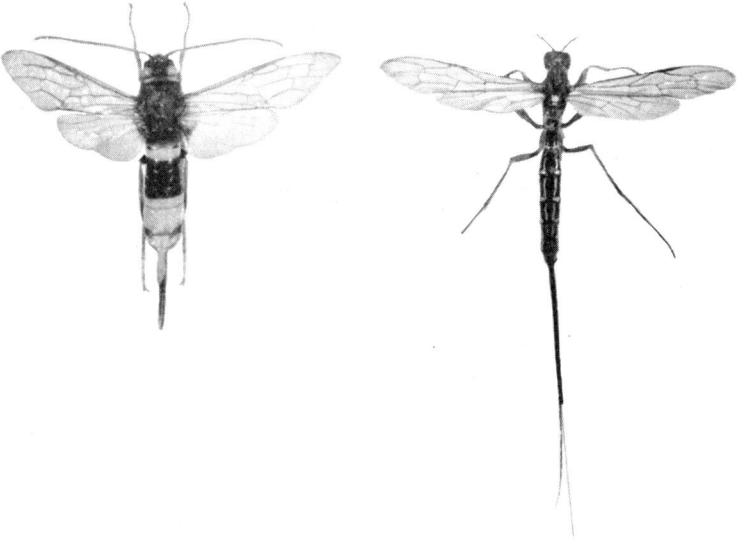

Giant Wood-wasp and its parasite. (*Natural size*)

parasitizes the Giant Wood-wasp. The latter creature spends its larval stages in tunnels right inside the heart-wood of logs from coniferous trees. Here the ichneumon fly has to attack its host, not by going into the tunnels itself, but by locating the position of the Wood-wasp grub from the outside, possibly by smell. Having found its prey it drives through the bark right into the solid wood its long egg-laying apparatus, which is even longer than its own body, and after much boring, reaches the grub and lays an egg on its body. It is not surprising that sometimes it makes a bad shot for, by the time the ichneumon has bored right down to the tunnel, an operation which takes perhaps twenty minutes or more, the Wood-wasp grub has moved along! Giant Wood-wasps are killed off every year in their larval stage by the ichneumon.

Ichneumon flies, even the small ones, are not free from being parasitized themselves. The kind that attacks Cabbage White butterflies—*Apanteles*—is itself the host for a smaller ichneumon—*Hermiteles*—which can somehow detect its presence even in the body of the caterpillar and drives its egg-laying tube

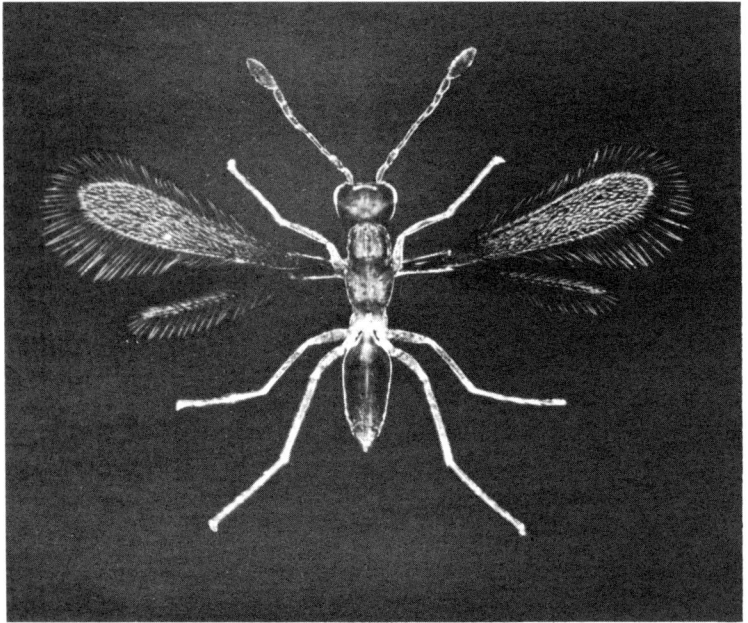

A Fairy-fly. (*Magnified*)

118

through the skin of the caterpillar to reach the larval ichneumon fly within! Even more remarkable is the fact that there are very small chalcid-wasps that parasitize *Hermiteles* so that in one caterpillar of a Cabbage White butterfly there may be a parasite within a parasite of a parasite!

Some of the chalcid-wasps, called the Fairy-flies, although extremely tiny and apparently completely unfitted for aquatic life, descend below the water of ponds and use their frail wings, which are fringed with delicate hairs, for swimming.

They search out the eggs of various aquatic insects such as water-beetles and lay their own eggs inside them. Their subsequent metamorphosis takes place in this unlikely habitat.

Other chalcid-wasps lay their eggs in those of land insects, particularly of moths, and careful investigation by one entomologist has shown that one chalcid, *Trichogramma*, uses the eggs of more than 150 different insects. He found that the female wasp, when laying her eggs, leaves an odour trail on the eggs of the host which can be detected by any other female wasp who happens to come along, so that she does not waste time laying her egg in the same place.

119

15

Waging war against insects

You will not be surprised, after reading in previous chapters of the damage caused by insects and the diseases which they transmit, that war has been declared on some of them and is now being waged ruthlessly in many parts of the world. Warfare is a most appropriate term for these operations; modern methods of controlling insects are often carried out with all the thoroughness and organization of a military campaign and the number of those taking part is often not far short of those employed in a battle.

Of course, it must be admitted that man has been responsible for causing many formerly harmless insects to become pests in the way mentioned on page 65 and, by his methods of modern crop cultivation, increasing their numbers to pest proportions.

Although man must always have tried to kill the insects that were troubling him or his animals it is only in the last fifty years or so that any considerable progress has been made in controlling insect pests on a large scale. This has come about by the accurate knowledge about insects—their structure, life-history and habits—that has been gained by entomologists; and by the development and wide use of a whole range of new insect poisons, or insecticides as they are called, which have been developed as a result of our general progress in technology, and in particular in chemistry.

INSECTICIDES

Let us consider first the various kinds of poisons that can be used against insects. Ideally an insecticide should be rapidly fatal to insects but harmless to other animals; it should be cheap as large quantities may be needed; and it should not produce any adverse effects when used in conjunction with the various liquids and powders with which it has to be mixed so that it can be used in spreading equipment such as sprayers. It is rarely that an insecticide with these three features is found, however.

Three distinct types of insecticide are employed: *stomach poisons* which kill insects after they have been swallowed; *contact poisons* which are lethal when they contaminate the insect's skin; and *fumigants* which act in the form of poisonous gases or vapours which reach the inside of the insect through its breathing mechanism. Perhaps we ought to mention here, also, *repellents* which are substances acting either by contact or by vapours they give off and merely keep insects away.

Stomach poisons include various substances incorporating arsenic, mercury or fluorine. An arsenical preparation called "Paris Green" has been widely used in mosquito control. The poison, diluted with a large quantity of some spreading material, is sprinkled by blowers over ponds where the larvae are living. The poisonous particles are swept into their bodies, along with their food, by their mouth-brushes.

Wood for building purposes is now often soaked under pressure with mercuric compounds to protect

121

it from damage by wood-boring beetles, such as the furniture beetle or termites. Woollen fabrics are treated with similar stomach poisons to protect them against the ravages of clothes moths.

Insects such as ants, cockroaches and earwigs can often be killed off when they have become nuisances by poison baits, foods liked by them being mixed with substances like sodium fluoride or sodium arsenite.

Contact poisons include pyrethrum, a substance obtained from the flower-heads of a kind of chrysanthemum flower. This must be one of the oldest known insecticides and has been used in the East for centuries. It still remains one of our most effective substances for it acts extremely quickly and is harmless to domestic animals, so that preparations containing pyrethrum are particularly useful for controlling household pests.

A wide range of oils derived from the distillation of coal tar is used, and insecticides incorporating creosote or anthracine are used widely as "winter washes" for controlling the pests attacking fruit trees.

A more recently introduced substance which has now become a household word is D.D.T., the letters being an abbreviated form of its chemical name dichloro-diphenyl-trichloro-ethane which gives some idea of the complex nature of some of these newer chemical substances! D.D.T. was actually discovered as long ago as 1874 by a student in the University of Strasbourg, but it was not realized then that it killed insects. It was not until 1940 when two Swiss scientists used it against the Colorado Beetle that its value was appreciated and its importance during the 1939–45 war in controlling insects and insect-borne diseases among the troops of both sides can hardly be exaggerated. It is rather slow in action and is extraordinarily persistent. Unfortunately, many insects have become immune to its effects and dangerous traces of it are left in the environment long after its application, so that severe limitation on its use has been advocated.

Another new arrival, not so persistent as D.D.T., is a substance called benzene hexachloride, a proprietary name for which is Gammexane or B.H.C. This has proved of value in this country in controlling wireworms and leather-jackets, two of the greatest pests of farmers, and abroad it offers great possibilities of solving many of the problems of limiting locust plagues.

Fumigants are usually employed to rid a house or building of such parasites of man as fleas or bed-bugs which creep into inaccessible places when not on their hosts. The most effective of these is hydrogen cyanide, a liquid which readily turns to a gas at low temperatures. As it is extremely poisonous to all living things the greatest care has to be taken when using it. A safer but less effective fumigant is sulphur dioxide.

The chief value of repellents is against insects which cause damage before any ordinary insecticide has time to act. Mosquitoes, for instance, can bite their victims in a twinkling of an eye and the damage would be done long before it would be possible to kill them with any kind of poisons. Repellents are substances which are strongly irritant to insects in some way. An old remedy in country districts for keeping both man and cattle free from biting insects is oil of citronella. The modern insect creams sold by chemists to prevent gnat bites nearly all contain the substance dimethyl phthalate, a colourless oily liquid used originally by the plastics industry, which has an almost magical effect of keeping insects off our skin if smeared lightly over exposed places, and was used a great deal during the last war to keep troops free of insect bites. It has one disadvantage: it dissolves certain kinds of artificial silk stockings!

Insecticides are mixed with powders, or liquids such as oils, so that they can be distributed easily by sprayers of various kinds or blowers. Sometimes, too, a substance called a "wetting agent" is incorporated so that leaves and other vegetation become thoroughly soaked all over with the lethal material. Where the areas to be treated are large, aircraft are used to carry out the spraying.

Naturally there are dangers in all forms of insect control. The substances used may be poisonous to man or his animals and great care must be taken to ensure that the edible part of the crops being treated do not themselves become tainted with the insecticide. Also, these poisonous substances do not distinguish between insect friends and foes so that pollinating insects, such as bees, parasites such as ichneumon flies that normally keep in check some harmful insects, and carnivorous insects, including beetles that also devour large numbers of harmful pests, are also destroyed by spraying operations. If used indiscriminately, therefore, even the best insecticide may seriously upset the balance of nature and undo what good it had achieved.

BIOLOGICAL CONTROL

Another method of fighting insect pests is by breeding their natural enemies, and releasing them in the affected areas. This is a method which has become of the greatest importance and has achieved spectacular success in some cases.

It has long been the custom in some Asiatic countries to use ants for controlling insect pests in orchards. But it was not until 1888 that biological control, as these methods are called, was used on a really large and successful scale. In that year a small ladybird called *Vedalia* was introduced from Australia to California to reduce the numbers of a scale-insect, called the Cottony-cushion Scale, which was devastating the groves of orange and lemon trees. Although only 129 insects were released, so quickly does the ladybird breed that within eighteen months it had brought the pest under control.

More recently the Giant Wood-wasp (mentioned on page 117) was accidentally introduced to New Zealand in timber from Europe and threatened to become a great pest of timber yards. Supplies of the large ichneumon fly, *Rhyssa*, which parasitizes this insect in its native haunts, were sent out to New Zealand and soon brought it under control and continue to keep it in check.

These two examples proved fairly simple in practice but sometimes difficulties arise in the use of biological control. For instance when the ladybird *Vedalia* mentioned above was introduced to control the same pest, the Cottony-cushion Scale-insect, this time growing not on oranges and lemons but on a plant called Spanish Broom, it was unsuccessful, as the ladybird was repelled by Spanish Broom and would not go near it even though its favourite food was sitting on it! Great care must be taken, too, that the introduced parasite is not one that will attack some quite different host in its new surroundings and leave severely alone the one that it has been sent out to destroy. There is also the possibility that the parasite may itself be preyed upon or attacked by a parasite, and all the care that has been taken in breeding it and sending it out is wasted. These problems, however, are being overcome as close study is being given to them by entomologists in the specialized research stations that exist for this purpose in various parts of the world. In Britain this work is centred on the Farnham House Laboratory at Farnham Royal, Buckinghamshire, where for many years there was a Parasite Laboratory collecting and rearing parasites of insect pests and sending them to all parts of the British Commonwealth of Nations. The funds for this work are provided by the various governments in the Commonwealth.

Insects are not the only creatures used to control their own kind. The Forestry Commission in Britain encourage insect-eating birds to nest in their woodlands, particularly in coniferous forests, by erecting nest boxes. These attract many more birds of the tit family to the acre than there would be without nest boxes. When it is remembered that a single pair of tits, apart from what they feed on themselves outside the breeding season, each bring a beakful of insects to their young during the time they are in the nest on an average every minute from perhaps 5 a.m. to 9 p.m. —a total of about 2,000 insects per day—you will see that the presence of birds in an area of woodland will reduce the insect population very considerably, although, of course, not all the insects eaten will be harmful ones.

In Puerto Rico, one of the West Indian islands, toads have been introduced to control an insect. These were no ordinary toads; they weighed two-an-a-half pounds each and are, quite appropriately, called the Giant Toad. The insect they were introduced to control was a kind of cockchafer beetle, the white larvae or grubs of which had become serious pests of the sugar cane plantations which are so important in the economy of the West Indies. The larva lives in the soil and feeds on the roots of the sugar cane plant, seriously hindering its growth and making necessary the replanting of the canes every year instead of every four or five years as is normal. In 1924 forty Giant Toads were introduced into Puerto Rico from Jamaica where they had been established previously, and after being kept in confinement for a time to make sure they would actually eat the adult insects, they were released and in ten years the beetle was so reduced in numbers as to be a pest no longer. Alas, it was then found that the toads were dying out and eventually it was found that aquatic insects were killing off its tadpoles in the ponds in which the toads bred. When this was realized small fish were introduced which preyed on the insects and thus the toad was saved. This example shows how closely interwoven is the whole economy of nature and how intricate, as a result, is the control of a particular creature. Who would expect to have to introduce a fish to control beetle larvae living in the soil!

16

Studying insects

If, as I hope, your interest in insects has been aroused through reading the previous chapters, you will probably want to know how you can study insects for yourself and so in these final pages I am going to try and show you how to begin.

In the past the "study" of any group of animals, and especially insects, usually meant killing them and building up large collections. Today naturalists are much more interested in knowing how animals live, and so it is the study of living insects that I am going to deal with in the next few pages. In the course of your investigations, however, dead specimens may come your way and so a short section will be added at the end to give some hints on making a study collection.

The equipment for any particular aspect of your study will be described as we go along but there are two really important items that are essential always and must be mentioned straight away. The first is a notebook in which to write all the observation and notes on the insects you are studying. Any cheap and simple notebook from a stationer or large store will suffice but it will be as well if it has a pencil attached. This notebook will be your "field notebook" for use when you want to make quick notes about any particular insect you have in front of you, whether it is, in fact, outdoors or indoors. As your study progresses you will probably find it an advantage to have also a loose-leaf notebook in which to write more careful and detailed notes and, by re-arranging the loose sheets, keep observations on particular insects all together even though they may have been made at long intervals of time. An even better arrangement is to keep the detailed records on little index cards which can be filed in alphabetical order, or under groups of insects, in boxes or filing cabinets. But the important thing about note-taking is that a rough book should be carried in the pocket always and that observations are recorded in it *at the time they happen and not from memory afterwards*.

The other essential piece of equipment for any naturalist is a pocket lens. This need not be an expensive one and there is available from dealers in natural history apparatus an item called a "nature viewer" which costs under five shillings. This is a plastic tube with a lens in the cap. A small live insect can be popped into the tube, the cap replaced and the insect examined without any fear of it escaping.

The most useful kind of lens, however, is the folding pocket magnifier with either a single lens to give a magnification of about 8 times or with three lenses each of which can be used separately to give a magnification of about 5 times, while used together they give increased magnifications.

Magnifiers of both types can be obtained for less than ten shillings from almost any optician or dealer in natural history equipment.

Carry a hand-lens always in your pocket or bag but when making observations it is an advantage to fasten a piece of string to it and hang it from the neck so that both hands can be free and yet the lens is readily available when required without fumbling in the pocket.

SILKWORMS

Perhaps the very best insects on which to begin the study of insects are silkworms, the caterpillars of the moth from which real silk is obtained. In rearing them through all their stages, from the egg to the adult moth, you will learn a great deal about insects generally. They are easy to obtain, even for readers who live in big cities. Eggs can be bought very cheaply from pet shops or dealers who advertise in natural history magazines, during winter or early spring. Two dozen eggs will be enough to start with. They will arrive stuck to a piece of paper and when you receive them put them into an unheated room or other cool place, although not where frost can harm them. If they were kept in a warm room during the colder months the caterpillars would hatch out before their proper food was available.

Silkworms are reared commercially on a diet of mulberry leaves but as few of us have access to a mulberry tree, lettuce will have to be used. As soon as the tiny caterpillars hatch from the eggs, which is usually in May, they should be lifted very gently with a small paint brush on to dry, tender lettuce leaves placed in an open box, such as a shoe box. There is no need to keep the lid on the box as the "worms" will not stray away from their food. At first the leaves will need changing twice a day and the caterpillars transferred to the new supply by very gentle use of the paint brush. As they grow it becomes tedious to move the silkworms by hand every time to new leaves and

130

a better plan then is to lay a piece of coarse netting from an old shrimping net or a string shopping bag over the leaves when they become stale and place the new supply of food on top. The silkworms will soon find the fresh leaves and when they have all passed through the net it can be lifted up and the dirt emptied out of the box. The next feed can again be placed on a net above the old one and the first net with its stale leaves removed when the silkworms have left it.

The important things to remember in rearing silkworms are to keep plenty of fresh leaves available; to ensure that the leaves are dry even if it means placing them between the folds of a towel before putting them in the box; cleaning out all the dirt from the container at least once every day; and keeping the silkworms in a warm place, but not in direct sunlight.

After about a week the silkworms will stop eating and they must be left severely alone for a day as they are shedding their skin. This moulting takes place four times in the life of the caterpillar as its skin has become too small for the rapidly growing body and a new one has to be grown underneath it. After each moult they make up for lost feeding time by eating more and quicker than they did before.

When they are full grown, silkworms are about three inches long, very fat and with powerful jaws which you can distinctly hear crunching the leaves on which they are feeding.

When they are at this stage they make good subjects for close study with the hand lens. Notice the strong jaws and watch them eating away a lettuce leaf. Notice too how the body is divided into sections or *segments* and in most of these on both sides you will see, if you look closely, dark openings, which are the *spiracles* or air-holes which you will remember are the structures

131

through which insects take in air for breathing. From there the air is carried along tracheal tubes (see page 24) to every part of the body. Observe that although the silkworm seems to have a lot of legs it has in fact only three pairs of real legs at the front of the body. The pairs of limbs at the rear of these are variously called false legs, claspers or pro-legs, which nevertheless help it to move along. You will remember that we said on page 8 that one of the characteristics of insects was that they had three pairs of legs.

PUPATION

Your silkworms will be full grown about the middle of July and you will notice that they then stop feeding and appear restless, often waving their heads from side to side. They are looking for somewhere to pupate and they should be removed from the box in which they have been reared and EACH placed separately in a cone made by twisting a sheet of stiff paper until it looks like an ice-cream cornet. To prevent the silkworm from escaping, the top of the cone should be closed by pinning the flap over. Inside its cone each silkworm will spin its cocoon of pure silk, usually yellowish or whitish in colour, and then change into a pupa or chrysalis. After about a week open one of the cocoons so that you can examine the pupa carefully. Notice the hard outer covering, which is protecting the developing structures of the adult moth. Notice too the silky cocoon from which you took the pupa, and then read again the section on commercial silk production on pages 80 and 81.

In about a fortnight unpin the flaps of the paper cones and place them in a deep box with a sheet of clean paper on the bottom. The moths will force their way out of the cocoons and flutter about in the box. They cannot fly so there is no need to put a lid on the box. After pairing, the females lay their clusters of eggs on the paper you have provided and very soon both males and females die and you will be able to set them in the way described on page 138. The moths do not feed in the adult stage so there is nothing you can do to keep them alive; their sole task has been to reproduce their kind. But they will provide you with useful specimens to examine and find out about adult moths: the scales which cover their wings, their compound eyes, their "feelers" or antennae, and so on.

In rearing your silkworm, therefore, you will have learned much more about insects and their development than you would ever have remembered if you had found out the information merely from a book. You will have seen the stages through which an insect passes from the egg to the adult moth—four in this case but as we have seen on page 13 other insects have only three stages. You will have noticed that the

Silkworm moths pairing. The eggs have been laid by another female moth. (*Photograph enlarged*)

caterpillar, or *larval* stage is the period of feeding and rapid growth and that the caterpillar has to moult several times to accommodate its expanding body. You saw that the adults did not feed but died soon after pairing. In fact, some butterflies and moths do feed on nectar from flowers which they sip by means of long coiled tongues. Through rearing your silkworms you will have become familiar with details of the structure of insects, their jaws, their spiracles or breathing apertures, the compound eyes and scale covering of adult moths.

Don't you think this is much more exciting than merely killing a butterfly or moth and pinning it into a cabinet?

REARING WILD CATERPILLARS

There is, of course, no reason why you should not try to rear wild caterpillars rather than silkworms if you live in the country or have a garden where the right kind of food plants grow. You will need something more secure than an open box in which to keep them, however, as they are much more prone to wander. The photograph shows a suitable rearing-cage made from a round biscuit or sweet tin and a roll of transparent plastic such as is sold by ironmongers as a substitute for glass. The edges of the plastic are secured with self-adhesive tape. A hole must be cut in the lid of the tin and a piece of perforated zinc or netting fastened over it on the inside. Perhaps you can get your father or uncle to cut the hole for you, or failing that a plumber will probably do it for a small charge.

The food plant is placed in a jar or vase of water to keep it fresh for as long as possible. When you find the

Rearing-cages for caterpillars. The one in the middle is made from a biscuit or sweet tin with a piece of transparent plastic between the bottom of the box and the top

caterpillars look carefully at the plant on which they are feeding and then you will be able to provide the right one throughout the caterpillars' development.

Butterflies and moths vary a great deal in their pupation habits. Some prepare cocoons on the food plant while others burrow into the soil and make a cell here. You will need to find out what kind of caterpillar you have by consulting one of the books mentioned in the list at the end of this chapter. Then you will be able to provide the right conditions for the insects to pupate. Suitable books will almost certainly be in your nearest public library or can be obtained by the librarian for you to consult. Read too in which month the adult butterfly or moth usually emerges from the pupal stage so that you will be ready for the exciting day when your specimens appear.

AQUATIC INSECTS

Another interesting group of insects for you to study are those that spend their life, wholly or partly, in ponds and ditches. Details of these were given in Chapter 8. You will be able to catch specimens by means of any kind of simple net.

It is usually better with the larger insects such as water-beetles, water-boatmen and dragonfly nymphs to bring them home packed in damp water weed in tins or plastic boxes, as they travel much better this way than actually in water in a jar.

At home a variety of improvised aquaria can be used. The wide range of plastic boxes now sold as food containers or sandwich boxes are ideal as they are shallow, and have well-fitting lids—a necessary precaution to prevent the inmates from escaping. A few stems of water plants and a small stone in each tank will provide shelter or support for the insects.

Once again, identification of the specimens will be necessary so that the appropriate food can be provided, and this should be easy if the books mentioned in the book list are consulted in a public library. Generally speaking, water-beetles, water-bugs such as the water-boatman, and dragonfly nymphs feed on animal food

Simple plastic aquaria for keeping aquatic insects. The long vessel on the right is an egg-rack which provides a convenient tray of 12 small containers for minute larvae. The brush and plastic spoon are useful for handling specimens

and will need small earthworms or tiny pieces of raw meat. Caddis grubs and China-mark Moth caterpillars need the leaves of water plants both to feed on and also to make their protective cases.

You can have endless fun and interest observing aquatic insects—the way they feed, the complicated methods they have to adopt to breathe atmospheric air although living underwater, how some of them eventually escape from the water when they have passed through their larval development, and so on. Don't forget to make notes of all the things you observe and when you have finished studying them *do* put them back in the pond or stream from which you took them.

Silkworms, wild caterpillars and aquatic insects are, of course, not the only kinds of insects you can study yourself but they have been chosen because they are good examples with which to begin and they illustrate the methods that can be applied with necessary variations to other groups. Further ideas for studying insects are given in some of the books listed on page 141, and to these I must refer you for my space is almost exhausted and there is room only to say a few words on setting the dead insects which come your way and on building up a specimen collection.

It is usual to set insects so that their legs, wings and antennae are all visible and neatly spaced. Different kinds of insects are set in a variety of ways but in nearly all cases a setting-board is needed. This is a flat board with a groove running along its length in which the bodies of the insects can fit while they are being set. Naturally, since some insect bodies are fatter than others, a number of setting-boards each with a different width of groove may be needed.

Usually the setting-boards are covered with a thin sheet of cork so that pins can easily be stuck into them. Although setting-boards can be made by anyone who is handy with tools, they are quite inexpensive to buy from dealers and your local natural history museum will be able to advise you where they can be obtained.

Other essentials are a pair of setting-forceps, two or three setting-needles in handles, a good camel-hair brush, a box of mixed white entomological pins and some strips of thin paper about 2 inches by 1 inch.

The illustration shows how a butterfly or moth is set. A pin held in the forceps is pushed vertically through the centre of the insect's thorax and stuck centrally in the groove of the setting-board. Using the setting-needles and perhaps the brush, the wings and legs are arranged in turn, the wings being secured by

Setting a butterfly. Strips of paper are holding down one wing, and the other is being arranged with a setting-needle. Forceps in the left hand are used to pick up and insert pins

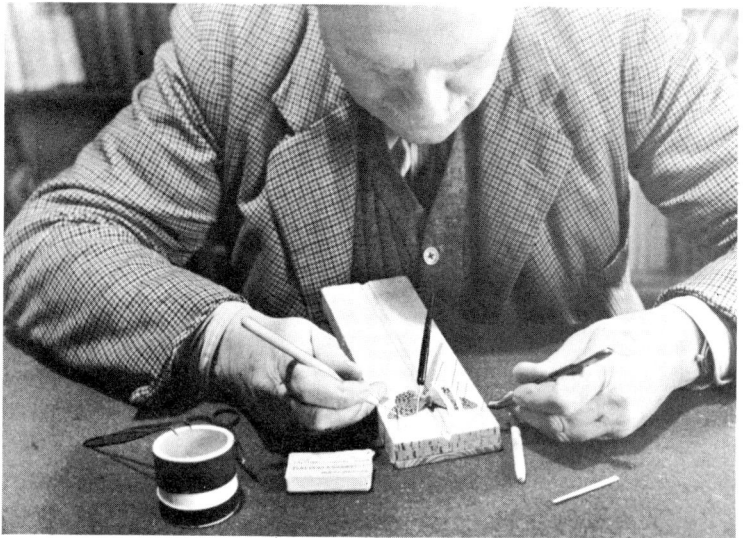

strips of paper held at both ends by pins, and the legs and finally the antennae by pins on each side of them. After a week on the setting-board the insect is then ready to be removed and pinned into a cork-lined store-box or cabinet. Beneath it, on the same pin, have a small label on which the following details are neatly written: date of emergence, where taken and your name. Another small label with the name of the insect can also be fastened on the same pin unless you are placing the insect in its final display cabinet straight away, when the label will be fastened below all the specimens of one species.

Should an insect have become stiff and rigid before you have had a chance to set it, relax it by placing it on blotting paper in an air-tight tin on the bottom of which is a layer of damp sand. A few drops of formalin on the sand will prevent the insect becoming mouldy while it is being relaxed. Formalin is obtainable from any chemist but do keep it away from your eyes.

Beetles and very small insects are usually set on small pieces of transparent celluloid or plastic. A thin layer of gum tragacanth (which any chemist will make up for you) is brushed on the celluloid, and the legs etc. arranged while it is liquid. When it dries it holds the limbs in place and becomes invisible. A pin pushed through the rear end of the celluloid will enable the specimen to be arranged in a cabinet or store-box and, of course, labels will be impaled below the insect.

Dealers sell "label lists" of most common groups of insects in which the names are printed and you can cut those you need to give your cabinet a professional appearance.

Finally, to prevent damage to your specimens by mites and other pests, a moth ball held securely by pins should be placed in the corner of each drawer of the cabinet, or store-box. Another method is to make a little bag of muslin and fill it with a few crystals of flake naphthalene (from a chemist) and pin that in the box. These substances all evaporate in time so they have to be renewed at intervals.

Store-boxes and cabinets can be bought from the dealers who advertise in natural history magazines. If you can, join a natural history society in your area, and you will receive help in your study of insects from more experienced entomologists. Your local library will probably be able to put you in touch with the secretary and will certainly be glad to help you find suitable books to enable you to read more about insects and how to study them. On the next page are listed a few books which you will find helpful.

And there we must leave the subject of insects. Perhaps this little book has made you think of these creatures in a different light: not as insignificant forms of life too unimportant to concern us, but as animals interesting and fascinating in themselves, of immense importance to human welfare, controlling as they do the destinies of nations and rendering some of the richest areas of the world almost uninhabitable, and yet in all their activities merely fulfilling a very important function in the intricate balance of nature which man himself so frequently tends to upset.

If a hundred readers of this book are tempted to delve further into the intricacies of the insect world, or merely one to emulate the example of the many distinguished entomologists who have devoted their life-work to add to the knowledge of insects which is now proving of such value to mankind, this volume will have been worth while.

Book List

In a small book of this kind it has been possible only to touch very briefly on many aspects of insect life. For further reading a selected list is given below of books which the author has himself found useful.

Most of the titles are inexpensive and those that are not are available in most public libraries.

Balfour-Browne, F. (1925) *Concerning the Habits of Insects.* Cambridge University Press

Bastin, H. (1956) *Insect Communities.* Hutchinson

Busvine, J. R. (1951) *Insects and Hygiene.* Methuen

Clegg, J. (1961) *Studying Insects.* Bruce and Gawthorn

Clegg, J. (1967) *Observer's Book of Pond Life.* Warne

Donisthorpe, H. St. J. K. (1927) *British Ants.* Routledge

Ford, R. L. E. (1963) *Practical Entomology.* Warne

von Frisch, K. (1954) *The Dancing Bees.* Methuen

Hirons, M. J. D. (1966) *Insect Life of Farm and Garden.* Blandford Press

Imms, A. D. (1947) *Insect Natural History.* Collins "New Naturalist" series

Linssen, E. F. and Newman, L. H. (1953) *Observer's Book of Common British Insects.* Warne

Mandale-Barth, G. (1966) *Woodland Life.* Blandford Press

Miall, L. C. (1934) *The Natural History of Aquatic Insects.* Macmillan

Newman, L. H. (1958) *Instructions to Young Naturalists—Insects.* Museum Press

Sanders, E. (1946) *An Insect Book for the Pocket.* Oxford University Press

Stokoe, W. J. and Stovin, G. H. T. (1944) *The Caterpillars of the British Butterflies.* Warne

Stokoe, W. J. and Stovin, G. H. T. (1958) *The Caterpillars of the British Moths* 2 vol. Warne

Urquhart, F. A. (1965) *Introducing the Insect.* Warne

Warnecke, G. (1964) *The Young Specialist looks at Butterflies.* Burke

The Amateur Entomologist's Association publishes inexpensive leaflets on methods of studying various groups of insects. A list may be obtained from the Publications Secretary, 1 West Ham Lane, London E.15.

Index

(Page numbers in italics indicate illustrations)

143

144